THE AGE OF UNREALITY

ESSAYS ON LITERATURE & TYRANNY

GREG OLEAR

FOUR STICKS PRESS

Paperback ISBN 979-8-9859319-5-2

Rise like Lions after slumber
In unvanquishable number —
Shake your chains to earth like dew
Which in sleep had fallen on you —
Ye are many — they are few.

— Percy Bysshe Shelley
"The Masque of Anarchy"

———

The Imperial need for control is so desperate because it is so unnatural. Tyranny requires constant effort. It breaks, it leaks. Authority is brittle. Oppression is the mask of fear.

— Tony Gilroy
Andor

———

Is this the real life? Is this just fantasy?

— Freddie Mercury
"Bohemian Rhapsody"

ACKNOWLEDGMENTS

———

This book contains 15 "Sunday Pages" essays, most published between Election Day 2024 and the Second Inauguration, edited and organized for this purpose.

Let me first and foremost acknowledge the wonderful and wise poets, novelists, screenwriters, essayists, journalists, artists, musicians, critics, and historians whose work inspired these pieces, and from whom I have learned so much. A complete list of cited material can be found at the end of the book. I encourage you to seek out their work, which will prove, I think, especially valuable in the Redux.

And I would like to express my humble gratitude to the supportive, generous, and lovely PREVAIL community, to whom this book is dedicated. Thank you.

We shall prevail!

PREFACE: YOU MUST GIVE TESTIMONY

———

As a nation, as a people, we cannot and will not heal until the Rough Beast and all of his thief-in-law accomplices are brought to justice. The psychic damage that Donald Trump has inflicted on us, and will continue to inflict for as long as the Redux lasts, is incalculable. His continued presence in our lives is nothing less than spiritual assault and battery.

The Biden presidency, which we hoped would decisively win the battle for the soul of America, proved merely to be a four-year lull, a Delaware speed-trap on the I-95 to tyranny, as insufficient as it was brief. All of Joe's many great achievements may as well be colorful chalk drawings on the pavement; the MAGA thunderstorm is washing them all away.

Not that we should be surprised. Disappointed, yes, profoundly—but not surprised. By the end of 2021, the writing was already on the wall. I wanted, we all wanted, not to translate the Dantean verse spelled out in bold letters before us. But there it was, penned in Merrick Garland's flimsy hand: *Lasciate ogne speranza, voi ch'intrate.**

In Italian it sounds so pretty.

From the moment that grotesque monster came down the gilded escalator in the tacky tower that bears his name, the news has been coming too fast to process, but also, paradoxically, not fast enough to bring relief.

This torrent of news brings to mind "Asphodel, That Greeny Flower," a poem by William Carlos Williams. Williams is best known for short verses—the 33-word poem about eating the plums in the refrigerator is probably his most anthologized work. "Asphodel," by contrast, is a long, rambling poem, a bit odd and hard to parse, written when he was 72, and supposedly about him confessing his infidelities to his wife as he lay dying.

Here is the end of the poem. I read this as a celebration of the power of poetry, which can—and which shall!—provide solace from the madness of the horrors swirling around us:

My heart rouses
                    thinking to bring you news
                                of something
        that concerns you
                    and concerns many men. Look at
                                what passes for the new.
        You will not find it there but in
                    despised poems.
                                It is difficult
        to get the news from poems
                    yet men die miserably every day
                                for lack
        of what is found there.
        Hear me out

---

*   Abandon hope, all ye who enter here.

> for I too am concerned
>
> and every man
>
> who wants to die at peace in his bed
>
> besides.

The key line: "It is difficult / to get the news from poems / yet men die miserably every day / for lack / of what is found there." The lack, that is, of what is found in *poems*. Art deficit. Literature dearth. Poetry famine. The quintessential MAGA complaint.

Never in my half century on earth has the future been more uncertain. And never before has the need for poetry, for art, for literature, for *beauty*, been so urgent.

I recall a 1993 poem by Zbigniew Herbert (1924-98) called "The Envoy of Mr. Cogito." Born in Lwów, Poland—now Lviv, Ukraine—Herbert had the misfortune of living under two brutal occupations: first the Nazi, and then the Soviet. That harrowing experience informs his work.

I can't pretend to know what the poem, in its entirety, means. But I have always read it as a meditation on grief, and on the need to continue to serve the greater good, even in the face of death. These lines, in Bogdana Carpenter's translation, I take as an instruction, if not an outright command:

> go upright among those who are on their knees
> among those with their backs turned and those
>   toppled in the dust
>
> you were saved not in order to live
> you have little time you must give testimony
>
> be courageous when the mind deceives you be
>   courageous
> in the final account only this is important

and let your helpless Anger be like the sea
whenever you hear the voice of the insulted and
  beaten

The poet Robert Hass wrote that Herbert was "an ironist and a minimalist who writes as if it were the task of the poet, in a world full of loud lies, to say what is irreducibly true in a level voice." Taking on that task will be vital to our survival during the Redux.

This book is a collection of some of my "Sunday Pages" essays, originally published at PREVAIL, most of them written between the 2024 election and the second inaugural—somehow just two weeks ago, as I write this. These pieces, and my decision to produce them as a book, is a concerted attempt to heed Herbert's command and "give testimony." Or, as William Carlos Williams puts it in "Asphodel,"

And so
                    with fear in my heart
                              I drag it out
and keep on talking
                    for I dare not stop.
                              Listen while I talk on
against time.
                    It will not be
                              for long.

———

—GMO
New Paltz, NY
February 3, 2025

CHAPTER 1
THE AGE OF UNREALITY

THIS IS NOT A MOVIE

January 19, 2025
One day before inauguration

———

THE GREAT BRITISH historian Eric Hobsbawm wrote an indispensable series of books in which he divides the 20 decades after the French Revolution into historical "ages." The period from the 1789 storming of the Bastille to the uprisings sweeping across Europe in 1848 he termed the Age of Revolution. Eighteen forty-eight until the end of the Great Boom circa 1875 was the Age of Capital. The Age of Empire spanned from the mid-1870s until the start of the Great War in 1914. And the "short twentieth century," a term he coined, was dubbed the Age of Extremes, and ran from the assassination of the archduke until 1991.

Ever since I discovered his books in 2012, the year of his death, I've often wondered what Hobsbawm would have called the fifth historical "age"—the one that began in 1991. That was the year of the first Gulf War, and the banishment from Saudi Arabia of Osama bin Laden that kickstarted his Al

Qaeda movement; the mysterious death of Robert Maxwell—friend to the British royal family, mentor to Jeffrey Epstein, business partner of the Russian mobster Semion Mogilevich, and Israeli spy—who fell off his yacht off the coast of the Canary Islands; the repeal of the apartheid laws in South Africa, where Errol Musk made his fortune; the rollout of the WorldWideWeb; and the breakup of the Soviet Union—on Christmas, no less, capitalism's holiest of holy days.

Today, a mere 24 hours and change before we hand the federal government off to a hateful confederacy of Nazis, mobsters, Opus Dei weirdos, white Christian nationalists, and billionaire dorks, I think I know not only the name of the period after the Age of Extremes, but also its termination date. As I type this, we are living in the last few hours of the Age of Unreality. It ends tomorrow at noon.

Something else happened in 1991, you see—something that likely eluded Eric Hobsbawm. Producers at MTV were developing a TV show that would begin filming in February of 1992. It was called *The Real World: New York*. It was the first reality TV show—or, at least, the seminal reality TV show of the subsequent reality TV explosion. Riding the reality TV wave was a British producer named Mark Burnett, who would give us *Survivor* in 2000, and, four years later, what wound up being the most historically significant reality TV show of all time, *The Apprentice*.

Although I confess to having enjoyed a few seasons of *The Surreal Life*, back when our eldest son was a baby—Flavor Flav does not disappoint!—I have never liked reality TV shows, encouraging, as they often do, the very worst of human behavior. I don't like meanness. I don't like ruthlessness. I don't like watching anyone being voted off the island. I don't like when people are fired. I don't like talentless humans. I don't like Kardashians. Most of all, I don't like the unscripted-but-very-much-scripted fluff that has replaced actual shows written by actual writers. By encouraging us to believe in a heavily-retouched fictional universe presented as the real world—or, I suppose, *The Real World*—reality TV has left us more susceptible to Russian disinformation, to deep fakes, to conspiracy theories, to manufactured media narratives, to tech-bro charlatans, to pseudo-scientific arguments against vaccines, and to mendacious politicians who have supercharged lying to a form of warfare.

I have often grumbled, half in jest, that reality TV would bring about the end of Western civilization. I did not think it would also bring about the end of Western democracy. To paraphrase Don DeLillo: Reality TV has given us Joe Rogan; that alone warrants its doom.

———

One of the most significant, world-altering events in this Age of Unreality was, of course, 9/11. In response to the WTC attacks, the FBI shifted its focus from transnational organized crime, which was already operating in the United States and growing more powerful by the day—a genuine threat to our society—to Islamic extremist terrorism, which involved not very many crazy people mostly living in caves far, far away from New York. In response to 9/11, we have to subject ourselves to TSA search before boarding an airplane. In response to 9/11, Bush and Cheney launched a long and expensive war on Saddam Hussein, who had nothing whatsoever to do with the attacks, while simultaneously cutting taxes for their wealthy benefactors—two actions that, in tandem, starved the U.S. treasury and put the country so far into the red that it may never recover. In Britain, meanwhile, Tony Blair's blind loyalty to Bush—a foreshadowing, perhaps, of Joe Biden's blind loyalty to Bibi Netanyahu— paved the way for BREXIT and the series of hapless prime ministers that followed the disastrous decision to LEAVE.

Five days after 9/11, Anthony Lane, the *New Yorker*'s

savagely witty film critic, published what remains one of the finest pieces of writing on the attacks, a short essay called "This Is Not a Movie." I go back and revisit it every once in a while, when the mood strikes me. Reading it now, I see that Lane perfectly articulates the paradox of the Age of Unreality, the uneasy blur between fact and fiction, when he comments on "the degree to which people saw—literally saw, and are continuing to see, as it airs in unforgiving repeats—that day"—that is, September 11, 2001—"as a movie." He notes that the elapsed time between the initial hijackings and the collapse of the north tower was "a little over two hours;" the length of a summer blockbuster disaster film.

Lane writes:

> What happened on the morning of September 11th was that imaginations that had been schooled in the comedy of apocalypse were forced to reconsider the same evidence as tragic. It was hard to make the switch; the fireball of impact was so precisely as it should be, and the breaking waves of dust that barrelled down the avenues were so absurdly recognizable—we have tasted them so frequently in other forms, such as water, flame, and Godzilla's foot—that only those close enough to breathe the foulness into their lungs could truly measure the darkening day for what it was.

There are echoes of this in the fires that have ravaged Los Angeles this week. Looking at those horrific images, it is impossible not to describe the fiery scenes as something from a movie—or, rather, a limited series, because, unlike with 9/11, the L.A. fires did not confine themselves to a movie-length running time. They began last Tuesday, almost two full weeks ago, and *are still ongoing*. If 9/11 was, as Lane suggests, a disaster film come to life, the fires are a combination of disaster film and horror movie: not just the fires themselves but the hundred-mile-an-hour winds and the dread of the fires spreading. *Only those close enough to breathe the foulness into their lungs could truly measure the darkening days for what they are.*

The fires are not a movie, just like 9/11 was not a movie. The fires are all too real.

As a country, we have not even begun to comprehend the extent of the damage, or its impact on all those hundreds of thousands if not millions of people in the Pacific Palisades and Altadena and beyond, much less the effect the fires will have nationally, culturally, societally—not least because the recovery will ultimately be overseen by an incoming administration not much known for its compassion, its competence, or its love for Hollywood.

———

The last paragraph of Lane's essay is achingly, hauntingly beautiful. Many, many people wrote about 9/11 in the days that followed that fateful Tuesday, and it always struck me as both unlikely and somehow appropriate that a film critic would offer the purest take:

> To be forced to disdain the ideal in favor of the actual is never a pleasant process. Even at its worst, however, it can deliver a bitter redemption. We gazed upward, or at our TV screens, and we couldn't believe our eyes; but maybe our eyes had been lied to for long enough. Thousands died on September 11th, and they died for real; but thousands died together, and therefore something lived. The most important, if distressing, images to emerge from those hours are not of the raging towers, or of the vacuum where they once stood; it is the shots of people falling from the ledges, and, in particular, of two people jumping in tandem. It is impossible to tell, from the blur, what age or sex these two are, nor does that matter. What matters is the one thing we can see for sure:

they are falling hand in hand. Think of Philip Larkin's poem about the stone figures carved on an English tomb, and the "sharp tender shock" of noticing that they are holding hands. The final line of the poem has become a celebrated condolence, and last Tuesday—in uncounted ways, in final phone calls, in the joined hands of that couple, in circumstances that Hollywood should no longer try to match—it was proved true all over again, and, in so doing, it calmly conquered the loathing and rage in which the crime was conceived. "What will survive of us is love."

Larkin, the poet who wrote that line—and who is, like Lane, British—was not at all a sentimental sort. His stuff is gloomy, sourpuss, almost defeatist. Throughout his poems we see a struggle between, on one hand, recognizing the futility of life, and on the other, being paralyzed by the fear of death. It is his poem "This Be The Verse," about how our parents "fuck us up," that the pub owner quotes, somewhat incongruously, in *Ted Lasso*:

Man hands on misery to man.
It deepens like a coastal shelf.
Get out as early as you can,
And don't have any kids yourself.

Sunny stuff, right? Larkin's entire worldview is neatly encapsulated in this line from "Aubade," a title that indicates this is a poem about the dawn:

And so it stays just on the edge of vision,
A small unfocused blur, a standing chill
That slows each impulse down to indecision.
Most things may never happen: this one will,
And realisation of it rages out
In furnace-fear when we are caught without

People or drink. Courage is no good:
It means not scaring others. Being brave
Lets no one off the grave.
Death is no different whined at than withstood.

The antecedent of the "it" in the first line is "death." But we may just as well substitute "Trump," and the lines work just as well: the standing chill, the furnace-fear and the rage, the necessity of other people and a good stiff drink, the futility of courage.

The poem that Lane quotes is called "An Arundel Tomb." At Arundel, a medieval British town, is the resting place of Richard FitzAlan, the tenth Earl of Arundel, who died in 1371, and that of his second wife, Eleanor of Lancaster, who predeceased him by a few years. The tomb is capped by stone statues of the couple, who are, surprisingly, holding hands:

Side by side, their faces blurred,
The earl and countess lie in stone,

Larkin, a dour librarian and bemoaner of the decline of civilization who seems not to have believed in love (even as he juggled three women for most of his adult life), calls bullshit on this romantic display:

They would not think to lie so long.
Such faithfulness in effigy
Was just a detail friends would see:
A sculptor's sweet commissioned grace

In other words, while the holding of stony hands has stood the test of time, the love it represents was probably a figment of the artist's rosy imagination. (Note the double meaning of "lie.")

How soon succeeding eyes begin
To look, not read. Rigidly they
Persisted, linked, through lengths and breadths
Of time. . .

Until,

Now, helpless in the hollow of
An unarmorial age. . .
Only an attitude remains:
Time has transfigured them into
Untruth. The stone fidelity
They hardly meant has come to be
Their final blazon, and to prove
Our almost-instinct almost true:
What will survive of us is love.

Larkin is saying that what the statues represent *isn't real*—that our "almost-instinct" is to believe in the much-bally-hooed power of love, and that the "stone fidelity" of the earl and his wife is so compelling as to make said love-power "almost true." *Almost* true is not true; *almost* true is AI true—a lie we want badly to believe in. The entire poem is him expressing his deep, nasty cynicism. The oft-quoted last line is intended to be ironic—a fitting epitaph for our Age of Unreality.

Even so, what survives of Larkin is "What will survive of us is love." And I like to think, as Lane does, that, whatever the poet's intention, the Arundel sentiment is real.

———

The Age of Unreality began in 1991, when all the ingredients of the historical cocktail were thrown into the shaker: the fall of the Soviet Union, the rise of the Russian mafia, the ascendance of Jeffrey Epstein, the dawn of reality TV, the end of apartheid, and the last time that a coalition of Western democracies repulsed an attempt by a despot to invade a sovereign nation—thus upholding the tenets of the Westphalian order. Out of that cocktail shaker, cold as ice, was poured Ghislaine Maxwell and Semion Mogilevich, Elon Musk and Peter Thiel, Vladimir Putin and Donald Trump.

Tomorrow, this mindfuck epoch draws to a close, and a new one begins. What it has in store for us is anyone's guess. Will the last barriers between fantasy and reality be worn away, or, as Lane poetically puts it, have our eyes been lied to for long enough? Will democracy really die, as the fascism scholars have been warning us for years, or will the Trump power-grab finally wake up the American people and restore our love of liberty? Will generative AI destroy all art, or will a new analog artistry emerge? What will happen to our beloved Hollywood, to which Trump has named meathead Sylvester Stallone, rightwing wacko Jon Voigt, and radical Catholic weirdo Mel Gibson his MAGA "ambassadors?"

I take some small solace in knowing that we've been here before. As Hobsbawm notes in *The Age of Capital*, the United States in the late nineteenth century—the America Trump wants us to return to—was marked by

> the total absence of any kind of control over business dealings, however ruthless and crooked, and the really spectacular possibilities of corruption both national and local—especially in the post-Civil War years. There was indeed little that could be called government by European standards in the United States, and the scope for the powerful and unscrupulous rich was virtually unlimited. In fact, the phrase 'robber baron' should carry its accent on the second rather than the first word, for, as in a weak medieval kingdom, men could not look to the law but only to their own strength—and who were stronger in a capitalist society than the rich?

The United States, alone among the bourgeois world, was a country of private justice and armed forces....

Our current crop of robber barons is orders of magnitude worse than its forebears—but maybe the abject awfulness of these despicable people will make their reigns shorter, their fall more humiliating, and their historical impact less profound.

Even so, for all my optimistic tendencies, I fear tomorrow as surely as Larkin feared death, which he describes as

The sure extinction that we travel to
And shall be lost in always. Not to be here,
Not to be anywhere,
And soon; nothing more terrible, nothing more true.

Death is permanent and absolute, but dictatorships are neither; moreover, Donald isn't a dictator yet, and may well never be. Even as I have witnessed the poltroonish capitulation of our political leaders, our robber barons, our media figureheads, even our Snoop Doggs, I have faith that we will somehow find a better way, that we will repulse this ugly MAGA incursion, that the moral arc of the universe will bend towards justice, that the better angels of our nature will prevail. My faith will be tested, surely. But it will remain.

Nothing more true than this: What will survive of us is hope.

CHAPTER 2
LES PROPHÉTIES

A BOOK OF QUATRAINS BY NOSTRADAMUS

Nov 24, 2024
Three weeks after the election

———

THE SECOND WEEK of June 2002 found us in the south of France. After spending the first view days of our honeymoon in Paris, catching up on sleep, fighting through the mosh pit in front of the *Mona Lisa*, being blown away by the Eiffel Tower (the magnificence of which no postcard could possibly convey), and drinking copious amounts of *vin rouge*, we took the train to Avignon, hired a reluctant taxi, and made our way to a little village, as old as it was delightful, called Saint-Rémy-de-Provence.

We were staying at a placed called Maison du Village, an enormous country house—also old, also delightful—that had been converted into what was technically, but only technically, a bed and breakfast. I chose it because it was 500 years old and teeming with the ancient charm of the *ancien régime*, and also because it was feline friendly. The estate was home to any number of cats, who had the run of the place—one of them was called Bowie, because, like the late rock star, his eyes were of two different colors—and I knew that after a week in Europe, we would be missing our own kitties.

The *maison* was a massive structure, even by today's standards, and in the sixteenth century must have seemed Versailles-like (although Versailles, of course, would not be built for another 150 years). It was nestled far beyond the road, and we drove to it by way of a long, arrow-straight driveway lined, as in some movie scene, by towering trees that may as well have been beefeaters standing at attention.

The plan was to get situated at the house and then get something to eat, as we were both ravenous. But while the Maison du Village is indeed within walking distance of the town, it's a good mile and a half away, and none of the restaurants in Saint-Rémy-de-Provence were open because it was three o'clock in the afternoon—including the one attached to the Maison du Village. This predicament we explained to the proprietress, who took pity on our honeymoon plight, repaired to the kitchen, and returned with two sandwiches—ham, cheese, lettuce, tomato, and butter, on baguettes—and a ceramic pitcher of chilled red wine. The combination of our intense *faim*, the mild panic about lack of provisions, and the astonishing quality of the food and drink that appeared as if my magic was beyond description. Twenty-two-and-a-half years later, that remains the best single meal I've ever had in my life.

———

The lone claim to fame of Saint-Rémy-de-Provence is that it was the birthplace of Michel de Nôtredame, better known by his Latinized *nom de plume*, Nostradamus. The Maison du Village, in fact, was said to have belonged to one of Michel's brothers. We had a running joke that instead of seeing visions of the future, this brother could only see visions of the past.

("Remember last Yuletide? Yeah, that was nice.") This was, I'll allow, more concept-funny than ha-ha funny.

"Nostradamus" sounds like a character from some fantastical work of fiction. Perhaps he is a talking rat in an animated tale, or a 36th-level magic-user that haunts some Dungeons & Dragons module, or an eccentric rich occultist who owns his own island, like Maurice Conchis in *The Magus*. He does not sound like a real person, and, unlike with most historical figures at his level of fame, I could not have told you, even two days ago, during which century he lived. But live Michel de Nôtredame did, without question: from his December 1503 birth in Saint-Rémy-de-Provence to his death, 62 years later, in Salon-de-Provence, some 40 kilometers away.

I tend to think of the sixteenth century as a sort of isthmus connecting the Olden Days to the Modern Times. The six decades Nostradamus walked the earth comprised a tumultuous period of rapid societal, cultural, religious, and geopolitical change. Gutenberg had invented the moveable-type printing press in the 1440s, so by the time Michel was old enough to read, books were available. Martin Luther nailed his *95 Theses* to the door of the Wittenberg church in 1517, firing off the starter pistol that began the Protestant Reformation. Magellan, who led the first expedition that circumnavigated the globe, set sail in 1519—the same year the conquistador Hernán Cortés began his war on the Aztecs *and* the same year that François I of France acquired the aforementioned *Mona Lisa* after the death of Leonardo da Vinci, of whom he was a patron. Copernicus reimagined the celestial order in *On the Revolutions of the Heavenly Spheres*, published in 1543. And so on.

Nôtredame's life was not a particularly happy one. Pestilence and plague followed him everywhere. His studies at Avignon ended abruptly when the university shut down during a pandemic. He was initially expelled from medical school at Montpelier for working as an apothecary—

dispensing cures to the sick. He married in 1531, and had two children, only for his entire family to be wiped out by plague in 1534. After finishing his medical studies, he practiced in Toulouse, in the heart of Languedoc, itself the heart of gnosticism. He married again and had six children. In Aix, he gained notoriety as a physician for successfully treating plague-riddled patients, and is said to have developed some kind of herbal remedy to ward off the disease. (For all his exposure to plague, Nôtredame never suffered from it, so maybe he was onto something.)

Michel believed, not without some reason, that there was a relationship between medicine and astrology. This is less cuckoo that it sounds; herbs achieve peak potency at certain times during the year, and Nôtredame thought that the calendar/remedy dynamic demanded more study. This led him, in 1550, to lean into his early interest in the celestial bodies, performed under the tutelage of his brilliant grandfather, and publish an almanac. This is what initially made his name.

It was during this phase of his life, halfway through the topsy-turvy sixteenth century, that he began having visions. He wrote down what he saw in cryptical quatrains—four-line rhyming poems with A/B/A/B structure. *Les Prophéties*, the fruit of this prognosticatorial labor, consists of ten sets, or "Centuries" as he called them, of 100 quatrains. It was with the publication of these books of enigmatical verse, in 1555, that "Nostradamus" was born.

The cockamamie idea of Nostradamus being gifted with foresight was cemented when Quatrain 35 of Century I seemed to predict the death of King Henri II, which makes perfect sense if you think this

Le Lyon jeune, le vieux surmontera,
En champ bellique par singuliere duelle,
Dans cage d'or les yeux luy creuera,
Deux classes vne, pour mourir mort cruelle.

The young lion will overcome the older one,
In a field of combat in single fight:
He will pierce his eyes in their golden cage;
Two wounds in one, then he dies a cruel death.

explicitly refers to the young French king dying after being accidentally wounded in a jousting match. Even so, prominent Frenchmen bought into the hype—enough so that even the rich and powerful nobility like Catherine de Medici regarded him as some sort of Provençal oracle. Did Nostradamus believe himself to be a prophet? *Absolument*! And he looked the part. With his Brooklyn hipster beard and piercing eyes, he was a proto-Rasputin.

My French is not good enough to remark on the quality of his poetry, but I don't know that anyone reads Nostradamus for its literary value. The pleasure of the quatrains lies in finding one that seems to accurately predict our present moment—although, for every relevant quatrain, there are 98 that could mean anything or nothing. This one is typical:

When twenty years of the Moon's reign have passed,
Another will take up his reign for seven thousand
years.
When the exhausted Sun takes up his cycle,
Then my prophecy and threats will be accomplished.

Like, okay, great, thanks for the heads-up, Mike!

———

But sometimes, like the proverbial broken clock, Nostradamus tells the time correctly. This quatrain is pretty clearly a vision of the United States, where we celebrate Thanksgiving on Thursday:

From the three water signs will be born
One who makes Thursday his holiday.
His renown, praise, rule and power will grow
On land and sea, bringing trouble to the East.

I have a slender Avenel Books edition of the Nostradamus prophesies, published in 1980, much abridged. I was flipping through it a few weeks ago in bed, to make myself more sleepy. Beneath each quatrain, in brackets, is what the prophesy is said to mean: *[D-Day, World War II?] [The Jews founding Israel despite British indifference?] [Roberts sees chemical warfare] [Leoni sees Spanish or U.S. popes or H-bombs!]* Retrofitting ancient cryptic prophesies to modern events is endlessly entertaining, and perfectly meaningless, and wonderfully unrelated to our slow descent into fascism.

But then I ran into one that gave me pause:

VIII. 20
Le faux message par election fainte
Courir par vrben rompuë pache arreste,
Voix aceptées, de sang chapelle tainte,
Et à vn autre l'empire contraincte.

False message about the rigged election
Runs through the city, stopping the broken pact;
Voices bought, chapel stained with blood,
To another, the empire constrains.

As I don't need to point out, Nostradamus seems to be talking about the here and now. "False message about a rigged election" is easily read as a reference to Trump's bullshit "Stop the Steal" narrative. "The city" is the internet. "Voices bought" are the chaos agents paid for by the Kremlin to flood the zone with disinformation. The "chapel" is the Capitol. "The empire constrains" is the weakening of the

United States that is a result of this. In other translations, the last line is "the empire goes to another," meaning someone undeserving of the honor, meaning Donald.

The next quatrain continues this theme:

Three foists will enter the port of Agde
Carrying the infection and pestilence of bad faith.
Passing the bridge they will carry off a million,
The bridge is broken by the resistance of a third.

The interpretation of this quatrain, in a 1947 edition I found online, is: "Agda, a city in France, shall be the entering point for foreign propaganda, eventually conquering the country thereby."

Foreign propaganda successfully conquering a country seems awfully familiar.

Oh, and in his epistle to Henri II, Nostradamus makes this prediction:

A great place will be established, with union and concord between some of the children of opposite ideas, who have been separated by diverse realms. And such will be the peace that the instigator and promoter of military factions, born of the diversity of religions, will remain chained to the deepest pit. And the kingdom of the Furious One, who counterfeits the sage, will be united.

The countries, towns, cities, realms and provinces which will have abandoned their old customs to gain liberty, but which will in fact have enthralled themselves even more, will secretly have wearied of their liberty. Faith lost in their perfect religion, they will begin to strike to the left, only to return to the right.

Secretly wearied of their liberty, you say? Return to the right? *Plus ça change, plus c'est la même chose.*

It's all bunk, of course. Nostradamus probably ingested a few too many of the wild mushrooms he was harvesting up in the mountains, and if he were alive today, he'd be picking football games on gambling podcasts, or predicting elections for *Le Figaro*, or producing some occult Netflix show.

Even so, there is comfort in prophesies, even baleful ones, because prophesies absolve us of complicity in the machinations of life. Who are we to resist outcomes already carved in stone? What hope is there for us, if all endings are predetermined? If nothing can be changed, why not just accept our lot and take solace in the fact that all things are beyond our control?

That fatidic comfort, I think, explains the appeal of organized religion. *Deus ex machina* is a beautiful thing. How blissful it must be, to believe absolutely that some divine entity is coming to save us! Or, for that matter, that we are capable of—or worth—being saved!

———

On our second and last night at the Maison du Village, we made the half-hour walk into Saint-Rémy-de-Provence for dinner. We strolled down the long driveway, shaded by the tall trees. We passed an enclosure where there were some dogs lying lazily in the afternoon sun. And we walked by field upon field of lavender, of which the summer air was redolent.

It was June, and we were farther north than we were used to, and I had observed that the sky didn't get really dark until about half past ten. So we enjoyed our dinner, and we had some wine, and then dessert, and then more wine. There were no cabs to be found, so we began to walk back around ten o'clock.

As it turns out, I had miscalculated the time of the nightfall. We were only halfway back to the estate when it suddenly got very, very dark. This was long before mobile phones came with flashlights, so there was no way of lighting our path. We clung to each other in the gloaming and doubled our pace, hoping that we would get to the driveway before the darkness swallowed us up completely.

The fields of lavender turned to black. There wasn't a living soul anywhere near us. And we were terrified—we, who lived in New York City, and regularly and fearlessly made journeys on foot more objectively dangerous than this.

At the turn into the driveway, the dogs in the enclosure came to life. They were barking at us ferociously, their yellow eyes gleaming in the moonlight, chilling us to the bone.

We practically ran the rest of the way, down the long dark drive, even the stars hidden from view by the shadowy treetops—the same path Nostradamus himself had likely taken, five centuries before: Nostradamus, who trusted that the sun would always rise the next day on those redolent fields of lavender, and who could glimpse the future well enough to know not to be afraid of the dark.

CHAPTER 3
WHO GOES NAZI

AN ESSAY BY DOROTHY THOMPSON

November 10, 2024
Five days after the election

———

FEW AMERICANS WERE MORE vociferous in their opposition to fascism than the foreign correspondent turned columnist and radio broadcaster Dorothy Thompson. She was the original head of Antifa—the O.G. "Auntie Fa."

From her press-box seat in Berlin, she watched as Adolf Hitler consolidated power in Germany. When, after years of futile trying, she was finally able to pin down the leader of the burgeoning Nazi Party for an interview in 1931, the article she wrote about the experience for *Cosmopolitan*, and the expansion of that article that became her 1932 book *I Saw Hitler!*, so thoroughly humiliated her subject that Hitler *personally* ordered her expelled from the country—the 1930s equivalent of being blocked on Twitter by Donald Trump. Talk about a badge of honor!

Here is a snippet of what she wrote about Hitler:

So I went to see not a little political leader, but a probable dictator "as certain to come to power as that I stand here," he had told some newspaper men a few days before. A man who owns an army. A man who terrorizes the streets. A man who predicts the constitution of a new dangerous, and awakened Germany.

I was a little nervous. I considered taking smelling salts.

And Hitler was late. An hour late. Waiting in the upstairs foyer of the Kaiserhof Hotel I saw him shoot by, on the way to his rooms, accompanied by a body-guard who looked rather like Al Capone.

Minutes passed. Half an hour....

When finally I walked into Adolf Hitler's salon in the Kaiserhof Hotel, I was convinced that I was meeting the future dictator of Germany. In something less than fifty seconds I was quite sure that I was not.

It took just about that time to measure the startling insignificance of this man who has set the world agog.

He is formless, almost faceless, a man whose countenance is a caricature, a man whose framework seems cartilaginous, without bones. He is inconsequent and voluble, ill-poised, insecure. He is the very prototype of the Little Man.

And, later: "Adolf Hitler's tragedy is that he has risen too high. In the seats of the mighty, the Little Man, lusty for power, nevertheless feels insecure."

It's almost like Adolf was triggered by a strong, confident woman calling him small!

And by eighty-sixing her from Germany, he was essentially proving her assessment of his gaping insecurity correct. "As far as I can see, I was really put out of Germany for the crime of blasphemy," Thompson remarked when she made it back to the States. "My offense was to think that Hitler is just an ordinary man, after all. That is a crime in the reigning cult in Germany, which says Mr. Hitler is a Messiah sent of God to save the German people."

Once home, Thompson became even louder in her antifascist advocacy. Example: She attended the February 1939 rally of the German American Bund at Madison Square Garden—the precursor to Trump's recent Nazi rally at the same venue. She sat up close to the stage and ruthlessly heckled the speakers, until security escorted her out. Nowadays this would be filmed on an iPhone and blasted all over social media under some clickbait title like "Watch this famous reporter EVISCERATE Nazis," but she had to make due with some photographs and newspaper coverage.

I should add that Thompson was, at the time, probably the most influential woman in the country, excepting Eleanor Roosevelt. She had great sway. Her words mattered. She inspired, and probably cajoled, her then-husband Sinclair Lewis to write *It Can't Happen Here*, his 1936 bestseller about a strongman taking power in the United States. She never let the fight go.

In August 1941—almost two full years after Hitler invaded Poland but four months before Pearl Harbor compelled the United States to enter the war—Thompson published a famous piece in *Harper's Magazine* called "Who Goes Nazi?" It's been making the social-media rounds again this week, for obvious reasons. She is an incredible writer. Her work is smart, insightful, and beautifully composed; her voice distinct. This is someone you wish you could go have drinks with and talk to about the world. As a frame for analyzing who goes to the Dark Side and why, she concocts in her piece "an interesting and somewhat macabre parlor game to play at a large gathering of one's acquaintances: to speculate who in a showdown would go Nazi."

What's so incredible about this piece written over eight decades ago is how on the nose it still is. Thompson constructs a dinner party, and takes us around the room, introducing us to the various attendees, and explains why they would or would not "go Nazi." Macabre, indeed.

"Nazism," she argues,

> has nothing to do with race and nationality. It appeals to a certain type of mind. . . Sometimes I think there are direct biological factors at work—a type of education, feeding, and physical training which has produced a new kind of human being with an imbalance in his nature. He has been fed vitamins and filled with energies that are beyond the capacity of his intellect to discipline. He has been treated to forms of education which have released him from inhibitions. His body is vigorous. His mind is childish. His soul has been almost completely neglected.

As I don't even need to point out, that accurately characterizes a healthy percentage of MAGA. Speaking of which, two of the gone-Nazi partygoers Thompson describes leapt out at me. First up, this jerkoff:

> I think young D over there is the only *born* Nazi in the room. Young D is the spoiled only son of a doting mother. He has never been crossed in his life. He spends his time at the game of seeing what he can get away with. He is constantly arrested for speeding and his mother pays the fines. He has been ruthless toward two wives and his mother pays the alimony. His life is spent in sensation-seeking and theatricality. He is utterly inconsiderate of everybody. He is very good-looking, in a vacuous, cavalier way, and inordinately vain. He would certainly fancy himself in a uniform that gave him a chance to swagger and lord it over others.

I mean, she even gets the *letter* right—the "D" here is clearly short for "Donald." And yes, there are trace details that aren't the same—Trump is not an only child; he was ruthless to *three* wives, not two—but it's still a spot-on description of the Orange Grover Cleveland.

But wait! Thompson also tells us about Trump's running mate, JD Vance, who is

> already a Nazi. Mr. C is a brilliant and embittered intellectual. He was a poor white-trash Southern boy, a scholarship student at two universities where he took all the scholastic honors but was never invited to join a fraternity. His brilliant gifts won for him successively government positions, partnership in a prominent law firm, and eventually a highly paid job as a Wall Street adviser. He has always moved among important people and always been socially on the periphery. . .
>
> He is a snob, loathing his own snobbery. He despises the men about him. . . But his contempt is inextricably mingled with envy. Even more than he hates the class into which he has insecurely risen, does he hate the people from whom he came. . . .
>
> There he sits: he talks awkwardly rather than glibly; he is courteous. He commands a distant and cold respect. But he is a very dangerous man. Were he primitive and brutal he would be a criminal—a murderer. But he is subtle and cruel. He would rise high in a Nazi regime. It would need men just like him—intellectual and ruthless. But Mr. C is not a born Nazi. He is the product of a democracy hypocritically preaching social equality and practicing a carelessly brutal snobbery. He is a sensitive, gifted man who has been humiliated into nihilism. He would laugh to see heads roll.

But inflation, amirite?

I remember the first time I read the piece, a few years ago, worrying that Thompson might classify *me* as a potential Nazi. (She has a way of writing that makes one want to meet her approval, even from beyond the grave.) As it turns out, irrational concern that a long-dead writer would peg you for a fascist is a strong indicator that you aren't one. "Kind, good, happy, gentlemanly, secure people never go Nazi," she assures us. "Believe me, nice people don't go Nazi."

That sums it up perfectly, right? The MAGA ethos, the entire Trump movement, can be distilled to those two words: NOT NICE. (What's the Greek for "rule by jerks?" Assholocracy?)

When I decided to write about Thompson for this week's "Sunday Pages," I knew nothing about her. The more I read about this marvel of a human being, the more I liked her— and the more I wish, frankly, that she were still alive. What a role model! Would that we were all as clear-eyed, as resolute, as unafraid.

I Saw Hitler! is only 35 pages long. It's of particular interest at this precise moment in U.S. history because the interview took place in 1931—before Hitler came to power, before the Enabling Act, before the invasion of Poland and Belgium and France, before the Holocaust. She doesn't view him as a monster, as we do (well, as those of us who aren't Nazis do). She views him as a twerp.

I encourage you to read the whole thing—again, the relevance of what she's writing about here cannot be understated —but here are some interesting takeaways.

First, the derivation of the party's name:

> The German nationalists were too reactionary. Their politics were those of the great landlord. The Nazis were aiming at the man who was like Hitler himself, the small middle-class voter. Socialism was international, and therefore, for them, anathema. But it had elements which he could use. Hence he called his plan national socialism.

And her accurate conclusion that the party's platforms are built on lies and nonsensical bullshit. Hitler's "social and economic theory is, to a halfway educated person, a tale told by an idiot. Compare it with Lenin's consequent communism and revolutionary program, glittering with intellect!" Thompson continues:

> But reason never yet swept a world off its feet, and Hitler, an agitator of genius, knows this. Self-interest, expressed in the most pathetic terms, does. Hitler is the most golden tongued of demagogues. Don't bother about the fact that what he says, read next day in cold newsprints, is usually plain nonsense. . .
>
> It doesn't, you see, makes sense.
>
> But if you want to gauge the strength of the Hitler movement, imagine that in America, an orator with the tongue of the late Mr. Bryan and the histrionic powers of Aimee MacPherson, combined with the publicity gifts of Edward Bernays and Ivy Lee should manage to unite all the farmers, with all the white collar unemployed, all the people with salaries under $3000 a year who have lost their savings in bank collapses and the stock market and are being pressed for payments on the icebox and the radio, the louder evangelical preachers, the American Legion, the D.A.R., the Ku Klux Klan, the W.C.T.U. [Woman's Christian Temperance Union], [anti-regulatory union leader] Matthew Woll, [the isolationist] Senator Borah, and Henry Ford—imagine that, and you will have some idea of what the Hitler movement in Germany means.

I don't need to tell you that Trump has done what Hitler did, in the same way Hitler did it, by cultivating the same constituencies that Hitler cultivated. And I shall be so bold as to predict that when he takes power this time, Donald will fully channel his inner Adolf, like so:

On the subject of the constitution Hitler was more explicit, though there again, I had to interrupt and address to an unseen gallery. "I will get into power legally. I will abolish this parliament and the Weimar constitution afterward. I will found an authority-state, from the lowest cell to the highest instance; everywhere there will be responsibility and authority above, discipline and obedience below."

So that's that for the Republic.

In *Words of Warning*, the biographer Peter Kurth writes: "Later, when the full force of Nazism had crashed over Europe, Thompson was asked to defend her 'Little Man' remark. 'I still believe he is a Little Man,' she replied. 'He is the apotheosis of the Little Man.' Nazism itself was 'the apotheosis of collective mediocrity in all its forms.'"

As Hitler, so Trump; as Nazi, so MAGA.

Thompson was right about Hitler being a Little Man, right about his insecurity, right about how he hated Vienna and socialists because the socialists he worked with in Vienna thought he was a weirdo and laughed at him, right about how the humiliation he felt at their laughter was the catalyst for everything evil that came later—rather like how thin-skinned Donald being brutally roasted by Obama at the 2011 White House Correspondents' Dinner activated the darkness inside him.

But she got stuff wrong, too. In the 1932 book, Thompson underestimated Hitler. She can see, plain as the (terrible mustache under the) nose on his face, that he was cipher, a loser, a weirdo. He was the Great Depression version of a creepy rightwing podcaster, a Nick Fuentes type. She saw it, and she assumed that because she could see it, everyone else could, too. *Ach, leider nein*, too many people could not see the Mark of the Beast in the Magic Eye picture.

Dorothy Thompson made the same mistake many of us, myself very much included, made in her assessment of the resident strongman: she believed the German people would be sophisticated enough to see through Hitler's grotesque lies, just like we all believed the American people would be sophisticated enough to see through Trump's. So confident was she in her conviction that the Germans would reject this little twerp that, as she sat in Hitler's salon at the Kaiserhof Hotel, she was practically laughing in his face.

In the end, things weren't so funny.

By 1932, Adolf had, like Donald, already attempted a coup and failed; unlike Donald, Adolf went to prison for it. Thompson writes:

> Mr. Hitler "sat" for a few months. As I recall it, he got a fifteen year sentence. But assassination and political conspiracy have been cheap in Germany during the past twelve years. He was out in a short time.
>
> Out, but somehow a changed man. Gone "legal." No longer was there to be a march on Berlin. The people were to "awaken" and Hitler's movement was going to *vote* dictatorship in! In itself a fascinating idea. Imagine a would-be dictator setting out *to persuade a sovereign people to vote away their rights.*

Ah, but Dorothy, we don't need to imagine it. We just did it. We *voted away our rights.* And very soon, "Who Goes Nazi?" will become more than just a parlor game.

CHAPTER 4
MEMORIAL TO THE MURDERED JEWS OF EUROPE

A HOLOCAUST MEMORIAL IN BERLIN

February 5, 2023
One year and nine months before the election

———

A SHORT WALK from the Brandenburg Gate, amidst the hustle and bustle of Berlin, is the Memorial to the Murdered Jews of Europe. Like Nazism, it sneaks up on you. One minute you're admiring the glass dome of the Reichstag Building; the next, you've stumbled into a warren of lugubrious concrete slabs the color of smoke.

This unassuming piece of prime real estate, an enormous city block, was once home to the wall dividing East and West Berlin. Designed by the American architect Peter Eisenman, the Memorial comprises 2,711 concrete slabs—or, properly, *stelae*—of various sizes, arranged in neat rows. They look like tombs. The cascading heights of the slabs, the fact that some are slightly askew, and the natural slope of the terrain underfoot combine to create an effect that is extremely disconcerting.

On the fringes of the Memorial, the first stela comes up to your knees—a manageable height. Then you start along the path, and before you realize what's going on, the slabs tower over your head. You think: How did this happen so suddenly? How did I not see this coming? Many Germans in the late 1930s, I'm sure, had the same thought about the rise of Adolf Hitler.

My friend who went with me to the Memorial said: "What makes this so powerful is that you don't need anyone to explain what it is or what it means."

How to reconcile today's progressive, artsy, creative Berlin —one of my favorite cities in the world—with the capital of a genocidal regime responsible for the systematic extermination of six million Jews? How can those two cities possibly be the same place?

For that matter, how does a nation—how *can* a nation— atone for the unforgivable sins of its past? In the United States, of course, we simply omit the shameful parts of our history. We turn the page and hope everyone forgets. We segregate Black history and honor it only during the shortest month of the year. We construct narratives that make heroes of slaveholding secessionists, that insist that the Civil War was about anything other than slavery. We decry "wokeness" and "CRT" at any honest attempt to teach the truth about the ugly institutionalized racism that has permeated American society since 1619. We pretend the insurrectionists were just overzealous tourists.

We dutifully preserve the Native American names of our towns and states and rivers and lakes, while ignoring the pesky fact that we actively tried to exterminate the people who gave those places such wonderful names. "Manifest destiny" was our pompous euphemism for wholesale slaughter.

Hitler studied what we did to the Navajo and the Chero- kee so he could do the same thing to the Jews.

We were the model.

In Nazi Germany, Jews were rounded up and killed. Romani were rounded up and killed. The disabled were rounded up and killed. Gays and Lesbians were rounded up and killed. Political opponents were rounded up and killed. Conquered peoples were rounded up and killed.

Nazis did that. That's what Nazis do. That's all Nazis *can* do.

Nothing can ever fully atone for what the Nazis did before and during the Second World War. But acknowledgement is the first step toward atonement. In Germany today, Nazis are rightly regarded with shame and horror; the Memorial is part of the reason why. In the United States today, Nazis are invited to break bread with the FPOTUS; our defiant historical ignorance *is* the reason why. Nazism appeals to the stupid, the petty, the artless, the cruel. It is, ultimately, a death cult.

So today, let us be perfectly clear: *There are no good Nazis.* All Nazis are bad, without exception—even Nazis who say they are rehabilitated, who claim to now be working for the good guys. There are no half-Nazis. To abet a Nazi—to platform a Nazi and allow him to spew lies, under the bullshit guise of "free speech"—is to become a Nazi.

In the summer of 2001, to raise funds for the Berlin Memorial, an ad campaign was launched in Germany. As the *New York Times* reported:

> "The Holocaust never happened" is the provocative slogan to appear in newspaper advertisements and on billboards starting Thursday seeking donations of $2 million for the Berlin Holocaust Memorial. Under the slogan and a picture of a serene mountain lake and snow-capped mountain will be smaller type saying: "There are still many people who make this claim. In 20 years there could be even more."

Twenty-*two* years later, and somehow, there *are* even more. For shame.

CHAPTER 5
J'ACCUSE...!
AN OPEN LETTER BY ÉMILE ZOLA

January 7, 2024
Ten months before the election

———

FERDINAND WALSIN ESTERHAZY, a slight man with a bushy mustache that looked like part of a child's Halloween costume, was a wastrel and a fabulist who bullshitted his way into the French Foreign Legion by exaggerating his credentials and pulling some family strings. He served without distinction in the infantry during the 1871 Franco-Prussian War. After blowing all his money during a subsequent four-year period of Parisian depravity, Esterhazy married, and immediately burned through his wife's dowry, spending money he didn't have on booze, dice, and bad stock investments. She left him in 1888. By 1894, he was in hock to any number of creditors, and so desperate he threatened to kill his wife and his children. With no other obvious recourse, he exploited his position of major in the army: he stole French military secrets and sold them to the hated Germans.

The treachery was discovered in 1894, when a housekeeper-cum-French spy who cleaned the German embassy found one of Esterhazy's communications—known as the *bordereau*—torn up in a waste basket. After a perfunctory investigation, blame was cast not on Esterhazy but on a military captain named Alfred Dreyfus. Never mind that Dreyfus was from Alsace—the beloved French region surrendered to Germany after the Franco-Prussian War a quarter century before—and thus more likely to detest than assist the Kaiser. Or that he was a loyal Frenchman. Or that he was innocent. He was a Jew in a nation of Catholics, and therefore the perfect fall guy.

In December of 1894, Esterhazy, who had clearly never read *Les Misérables*, watched silently as Dreyfus was convicted of the crime *he* committed—treason—and sentenced to life imprisonment on the South American French penal colony of Devil's Island, which was just as miserable as the name implies. Two years later, the head of French counterintelligence discovered new evidence, opened an investigation, and determined that Dreyfus was innocent and Esterhazy the real culprit. This evidence was suppressed by the military brass, the counterintelligence guy was reassigned, and Esterhazy, after a speedy and corrupt trial at which fake documents were introduced as evidence, was acquitted.

By 1896, the French public was well aware of, and deeply divided over, the Dreyfus Affair. The "Dreyfusards," who supported the falsely accused captain, included everyone of consequence in French artistic circles, including the actor Sarah Bernhardt, the poet Charles Péguy, and the writer Anatole France; on the other side was the editor of a virulently antisemitic newspaper. (Note: If the artists are all on one side of an issue, that's the side you want to be on.)

But it was the novelist Émile Zola who thrust the scandal into the spotlight, with his open letter to the president of France, which ran on the front page of the French newspaper *L'Aurore* on January 13, 1898—126 years ago this week—

under the now-famous banner headline "*J'Accuse...!*" Over the course of some 5,000 words, Zola dismantles the case against Dreyfus, calls out the military men who covered up for Esterhazy, and accuses all involved of corruption and anti-semitism.

In the final paragraphs of the piece, Zola writes, in words eerily relevant to the Trump era United States:

Where is that truly strong, judiciously patriotic administration that will dare to clean house and start afresh? How many people I know who, faced with the possibility of war, tremble in anguish knowing to what hands we are entrusting our nation's defense! And what a nest of vile intrigues, gossip, and destruction that sacred sanctuary that decides the nation's fate has become! We are horrified by the terrible light the Dreyfus affair has cast upon it all, this human sacrifice of an unfortunate man, a "dirty Jew." Ah, what a cesspool of folly and foolishness, what preposterous fantasies, what corrupt police tactics, what inquisitorial, tyrannical practices! What petty whims of a few higher-ups trampling the nation under their boots, ramming back down their throats the people's cries for truth and justice, with the travesty of state security as a pretext.

Indeed, it is a crime to have relied on the most squalid elements of the press, and to have entrusted Esterhazy's defense to the vermin of Paris, who are now gloating over the defeat of justice and plain truth. It is a crime that those people who wish to see a generous France take her place as leader of all the free and just nations are being accused of fomenting turmoil in the country, denounced by the very plotters who are conniving so shamelessly to foist this miscarriage of justice on the entire world. It is a crime to lie to the public, to twist public opinion to insane lengths in the service of the vilest death-dealing machinations. It is a crime to poison the minds of the meek and the humble, to stoke the passions of reactionism and intolerance, by appealing to that odious anti-Semitism that, unchecked, will destroy the freedom-loving France of the Rights of Man. It is a crime to exploit patriotism in the service of hatred, and it is, finally, a crime to ensconce the sword as the modern god, whereas all science is toiling to achieve the coming era of truth and justice.

Truth and justice, so ardently longed for! How terrible it is to see them trampled, unrecognized and ignored!

I quote from *"J'Accuse...!"* now because, in the event of Trump's re-election and subsequent weaponization of the Justice Department and the courts to punish his enemies, this is the sort of disgusting corruption—exacerbated by the same ugly antisemitism that is now escalating in the United States in the wake of October 7—we can expect to see in the despotic reign of Donald the Stinky.

For his trouble, Zola was sued for libel, lost, and was forced to flee to England—where Esterhazy, shorn of his bushy mustache, had also fled. Preposterous libel cases against writers, with corrupt outcomes, are also on the menu in a second Trump term, as promised by his attack dog Kash Patel. Are we all to flee to England?

After his return from exile in 1899, Zola was the target of a number of assassination attempts. The reactionary French military, bound by a fascistic strain of radical Catholicism, had many ardent supporters in the country, many of them keen to do violence. We might call them *"le MAGA."* God only knows how many people were scared into silence by the fear of physical injury.

Dreyfus, eager to move on with his life, took a pardon. He returned to the military and served honorably during the four years of the Great War—as if to prove that he was no stinking traitor.

In 1902, the zealots got Zola. An anti-Dreyfus workman

was paid to block up his chimney, and on the cold night of September 29, the writer died in his sleep of carbon monoxide poisoning. He was 62. And for all his many novels, for all his influence on the naturalist literary movement, what he is best known for is that open letter, in which he denounces anti-semitism, speaks truth to power, and demands justice for all.

As the second article of the Declaration of the Rights of Man lays out—in words easy enough for English speakers to understand, although they are in French—the natural and inalienable rights are: *la liberté, la propriété, la sûreté et la résistance à l'oppression.*

Let it always be so.

CHAPTER 6
CASABLANCA
A FILM BY MICHAEL CURTIZ

April 28, 2024
Six months before the election

———

THE FIRST TIME I saw *Casablanca* was in 1992, at the Key Theatre, a now-defunct arthouse cinema on Wisconsin Avenue in Georgetown, at a special theatrical release celebrating the film's 50th anniversary. The most recent time I saw *Casablanca* was last night. In between, I've seen it probably two dozen times. On each viewing, I notice something I hadn't seen before, walk away with something new.

Casablanca is often described as a romance—and it is. Bogart and Bergman are one of the all-time Hollywood pairings, and, "Here's looking at you, kid," is probably the film's best known line. The conflict in romances derives from the insurmountability of the obstacle, on what is keeping the two lovers apart: Romeo and Juliet are the teenage kids of two families in a blood feud; Harry and Sally don't want to risk their friendship for a romantic engagement that might not work out; Tom Hanks lives in Baltimore and Meg Ryan lives in Seattle. The obstacle in *Casablanca* is realistic, tragic, and completely insurmountable. It is a riddle that cannot be solved, a problem that has no solution, like how to fix the United States while the Senate exists.

But *Casablanca* is not just a romance. It is a drama. It is a war film. It is a buddy movie, replete with some of the sharpest comic dialogue ever written. It is a heist picture—we don't see the two German couriers murdered on the train, we don't see the letters of transit stolen from them, but the rush to obtain those two documents animates one of cinema's greatest plots. It is an exploration of how to deal with heartbreak and loss. It is a story about sacrifice and courage and redemption and standing up to tyranny. It is an allegory for a world that, when it was made in 1942, was very much still at war—and, as such, is an overtly political film. *Casablanca* contains multitudes.

When I first watched the movie, I was more concerned with the romantic content. I loved Rick, loved his café, loved his white tuxedo jacket and his gruff manner and how he threw the best party but always held himself at a remove. But it is impossible to watch *Casablanca* in 2024 and not focus on the Nazis.

The first action we see in *Casablanca* is a violent police crackdown. And not just any violent police crackdown. This part of North Africa is controlled by unoccupied France, the German rump state based in Vichy. A prominent Nazi is coming to town, and the local authorities are detaining all the potential rabble-rousers—the usual suspects, as it were—who might not welcome the Gestapo's jackbooted presence in French Morocco. One fellow is menaced by the police, who shoot and kill him when he tries to resist arrest; when they search his body, they find he is carrying leaflets for Free France.

If the film were made today, this scene would have been shot on location, in Casablanca or a city that could reasonably pass as Casablanca, and the terror of the crackdown would be amplified in one of those grandiose action scenes that modern movies often open with. But the film was produced in 1942. It was shot on a soundstage in Hollywood. The danger is cloaked behind old-timey cinematic production. No matter. The opening distinctly shows brutal, Nazi-aligned cops using unnecessary force, shooting and killing an agent of the Resistance: an anti-Fascist.

Similarly, the first time we see Rick—after we meet Captain Renault, the French prefect of police, and Major Strasser, the Nazi big wheel—he is alone at a chess board in the casino part of the club. His first lines of dialogue are directed to an arrogant Nazi—an official at Deutsche Bank, no less!—whom he bars from entering the inner sanctum:

—Your cash is good at the bar.
—What? Do you know who I am?
—I do. You're lucky the bar's open to you.

Rick owns and manages the café, and he is a good boss. He supports his employees, reassuring Emil after the house loses 20,000 francs, and keeping everyone on the payroll when the police shut him down. But he keeps himself aloof. "I stick my neck out for no one," he says when the police arrest Ugarte. "I'm the only cause I'm interested in," he tells Ilsa. But this is a false front, a defense mechanism. He doesn't want his heart broken again. He is, as Victor Laszlo astutely observes, a man trying to convince himself of something he doesn't really believe.

At 17 and a half minutes into the movie, Ferrari, criminal overlord and owner of the Blue Parrot, remarks to Rick that "isolationism is no longer a practical policy." That line may as well have been spoken to the entire country. Rick and Sam, his friend and piano player, are the only Americans in *Casablanca*, and as such, represent the United States. The staff and clientele at his club come from everywhere: Carl is an anti-Nazi German, Sascha is Russian, Emil and Yvonne are French, Abdul is Moroccan, Berger is Norwegian, and so on. In that sense, the café is a microcosm of Europe. (In real life, many of the supporting actors were European war refugees who had escaped the actual Nazis—including the astonishingly good actor who plays the Gestapo's Major Strasser, Conrad Veidt, who fled his native country with his Jewish wife when Hitler came to power.)

It is no accident that the action in *Casablanca* takes place over three days in early December, 1941—just before Pearl Harbor. Rick, like the U.S. in the late fall of 1941, preferred to remain neutral. But ultimately, like the U.S., he is drawn into the fight—and his presence ultimately helps the good guys prevail.

Perhaps the film's most rousing scene is when the orchestra, with its brass instruments, overpowers the Germans singing patriotic songs at the piano, with a stirring rendition of "La Marseillaise," the French national anthem. In 1992, I chalked it up to Hollywood schlock; now, I recognize the scene's awesome power: music becomes the field of battle. Even Yvonne, last seen flirting with a handsome Nazi, is moved to tears.

But the film is not all doom and gloom. *Casablanca* rewards us with sharp dialogue and genuinely funny moments. When Victor Laszlo arrives at Rick's, he orders drinks, only to have his orders upgraded and put on someone else's tab, which annoys him; it's a running joke that he can't pay for his own drink. Carl's aside with the couple practicing their English before leaving for America is comic gold. And as Captain Renault, Claude Reins drops one-liner after one-liner, in a remarkably modern performance—not least of which the famous "I'm shocked, shocked" scene.

When Rick sits down for his interrogation by the Nazis, he is asked his nationality. "I'm a drunkard," he says dryly—and it looks like the men at the table are genuinely laughing, as if the line was ad-libbed. But Renault immediately supplies the rejoinder: "And that makes Rick a man of the world."

We learn that what causes Rick's moral paralysis is his heartbreak. Ilsa Lund—the wife and traveling companion of the Resistance leader Victor Laszlo, who has just arrived in town—is, improbably, the woman who broke his heart. The chances of them meeting again like this are a million to one, which Rick alludes to in yet another famous line: "Of all the gin joints in all the towns in all the world, she walks into mine."

During their confrontation later in the film, Ilsa accuses him of, basically, nurturing a grievance: "You want to feel sorry for yourself, don't you? With so much at stake, all you can think of is your own feelings. One woman has hurt you, and you take your revenge on the rest of the world. You're a coward and a weakling." She may as well be addressing Elon Musk, or any one of a thousand other alt-right Twitter incels.

But by then, Rick has already started to change. Precedents are being broken. He's having a drink with customers now. He's involving himself in politics more overtly. This is made clear in the scene with the Bulgarian refugee, Annina. She is, Rick observes, underage and should not be at the bar. But she seeks him out. She wants to be reassured, without explicitly saying so, that if she has sex with Captain Renault, he will honor his promise and let her and her husband leave for America. This is dark, dark stuff, concealed by the soft lighting and the beautiful actress:

> Oh, monsieur, you are a man. If someone loved you very much, so that your happiness was the only thing that she wanted in the world—but she did a bad thing to make certain of it—could you forgive her?

Rick replies with a punch to the gut: "No one ever loved me that much."

But this is not true, although he doesn't realize it yet. Ilsa did love him that much. And he is sufficiently moved by Annina to arrange for her husband to win at roulette, securing enough money to finance their visas—much to the delight of the staff.

The first time I saw the movie, I knew what the last line was, so I had some idea of the ending, but I didn't know anything else. Twenty minutes from the end, Rick gives Victor Laszlo the letters of transit. Renault emerges from the shadows to arrest him. And I remember thinking, "Holy shit! How the hell are they going to resolve this?" I wasn't the only one. Even the *screenwriters* didn't know, well after production began. All they did was devise the best ending of all time.

We think Rick and Ilsa will take the letters of transit and leave. Ilsa thinks that, too. But that's not what happens. Once at the airport, Rick informs Renault that *Ilsa and Victor* will be the ones leaving. This surprises Ilsa, Renault—and the audience. But this is Rick putting away his personal grievance for the greater good. This is him atoning for the sins of the past. This is also him entering the fray, as Laszlo tells him on the tarmac, in a line I use in the intro to my podcast: "Welcome back to the fight. This time, I know our side will win." That line is spoken in December of 1941—for all we know, Japanese planes are bombing Pearl Harbor *as* Laszlo's plane flies to Lisbon. If Rick represents America, this is America entering the war. And, remember, the movie came out in 1942! "Our side" winning was *not* a sure thing.

(Also: Rick told Victor that the letters of transit were not for sale at any price. At the end, he refuses to take Victor's money—which both makes the comment about the letters not being for sale true, and also continues the running joke about Laszlo not being able to pay for his own drinks.)

The Resistance leader and his wife get on the plane. The

plane taxis out to the strip. And then, the Nazi big wheel shows up! After warning him to put down the phone, Rick shoots and kills him. Renault explains how "unpleasant" this is going to be. "I'll have to arrest you, of course."

The plane takes off, heading for Lisbon. The couple makes it out of Casablanca. Rick wins his 10,000 franc bet with Renault.

Then the police show up.

And watching the movie, we prepare for Rick's impending arrest. "Major Strasser has been shot," Renault tells his charges.

And there is a long, dramatic pause, before he delivers yet another of the film's famous lines: "Round up the usual suspects." With those five words, he lets Rick go free.

Renault—an unscrupulous lech who "blows with the wind," a "poor, corrupt official" who exploits his authority by bedding desperate refugee women—has found his own way back to the light. He, too, is back in the fight. And he and Rick leave together, bound for the French garrison at Brazzaville, and adventures to come, and a continuation of what is already a beautiful friendship.

Watching the film again last night, there was something else I realized about *Casablanca*. No one wants to be in Morocco. Everyone wants to go to America. The word is spoken countless times: America, America, America. Rick is American but can't go back to America, although he desperately wants to. America is the symbol of freedom, of safety, of security, of respite from the Third Reich. The entire black market of French Morocco revolves around guarantees of safe passage to America. It's taken as a given that America is the land of the free.

But now, somehow, 82 years after the release of *Casablanca*, this is no longer the case. Nazis are again on the rise—only this time, they're not in Europe or North Africa but here, in America, among us. What would those supporting actors who fled the Third Reich have made of that? What would Rick have thought?

While helping dress his wound, Rick asks Victor if he thinks what he's fighting for—that is, democracy, freedom, anti-fascism—is worth it. I leave you with Laszlo's response: "You might as well question why we breathe. If we stop breathing, we'll die. If we stop fighting our enemies, the world will die."

The fundamental things apply, as time goes by.

CHAPTER 7
THE UNBEARABLE LIGHTNESS OF BEING
A NOVEL BY MILAN KUNDERA

February 25, 2024
Nine months before the election

———

MILAN KUNDERA, the great Czech-born French novelist, died this past July at the age of 94.

His father was a prominent musician who ran the Janáček Academy of Performing Arts, and for a while, it seemed like Milan would follow in his footsteps. But 1929 was a bad time to be born in Czechoslovakia. Kundera entered the world during the progressive, democratic First Czechoslovak Republic. He was four years old when the Nazis took control of Germany, Central Europe's hegemonic power post-World War One, leaving his small country the lone democracy in the region. He was nine during the Sudetenland crisis, nine and a half when Chamberlain promised "peace in our time," a month shy of ten when the Czech government collapsed and became a Nazi rump state (the very Third Reich-sounding Protectorate of Bohemia and Moravia), and ten and a half when Hitler invaded Poland.

After the war, his country had the misfortune of being "liberated" by the Soviets, which merely transferred the Czech lands from the yoke of one homicidal madman to another. As a student, Kundera was an ardent Communist—the underlying concept of "we should all share resources so there is no want" is more appealing to young people with artistic tendencies than the zero-sum nastiness of unbridled capitalism—but he soon realized that the Marxist paradise he was promised did not, and could never, exist.

Kundera was not an activist in the way we understand the term. The more overtly political Czech writer of international renown was the playwright Václav Havel, and the two men did not get along, famously arguing about the efficacy of political protest. They were the Biggie and Tupac of the Czech literary scene. Their point of contention is summed up neatly by Benjamin Herman in his essay, "The Debate That Won't Die: Havel And Kundera On Whether Protest Is Worthwhile":

> Does waging a public protest against a much more powerful oppressor serve any purpose if it is certain that the protest will (1) fail to attain its stated goal and (2) hurt the protester and his family? And if failure is certain, isn't it possible that the protester's primary motive is actually to make himself look heroic?

No, Kundera concludes. Havel calls bullshit on Kundera's "pseudo-critical illusionism." Kundera then accuses Havel of "moral exhibitionism." (Havel wound up serving as the first president of the Czech Republic, which probably awards him the win in this particular debate.)

But Kundera chafed nonetheless under Communist rule, as brutal and soul-crushing as it was banal and stupid. He was expelled from the Communist Party in 1950. His books were banned in 1968, the year of the Prague Spring, the ever-so-brief attempt by Czechoslovakia to stand up to Russian tyranny. At the urging of his friend, the French publisher Claude Gallimard, he moved to France in 1975. Four years later, Czechoslovakia revoked his citizenship. He lived the rest of his long life in Paris, an eminent writer in reluctant exile.

I didn't know any of this when I first read *The Unbearable Lightness of Being*—Kundera's best-known work, published in 1984, when he was 53—in 1992. I was a sophomore in college, an English major, and it was a novel that was fashionable, probably because the film had come out a few years prior.

What do I remember about that first encounter with *The Unbearable Lightness of Being*? Not much. The protagonist was a womanizing doctor-turned-window washer. There were philosophical flourishes. And there was the sexy woman in the bowler hat—the anachronistic haberdasherian fashion accessory that graces almost every cover of every edition of the book. The mental image I cooked up of Sabina in her lingerie and that hat was seared into my 19-year-old brain, an icon (in the Byzantine and not the social media sense) of literary eroticism.

I also remember this remarkable passage, which I still think about whenever I am high up in a Ferris wheel or an skyscraper's observation deck:

> Anyone whose goal is something higher must expect someday to suffer vertigo. What is vertigo? Fear of falling? Then why do we feel it even when the observation tower comes equipped with a sturdy handrail? No, vertigo is something other than the fear of falling. It is the voice of the emptiness below us which tempts us and lures us, it is the desire to fall, against which, terrified, we defend ourselves.

I had intended to write about Kundera right after he died, so I am more than half a year late. But I knew that to do his memory any justice, I had first to re-read *The Unbearable Lightness of Being*. Would I, at age 51, find more in it than I did at 19?

The answer is a resounding *Absolutně*. For all the aforementioned philosophical flourishes so appealing to a college humanities student—the musings about eternal recurrence; the Parmenides catalog of opposites that give the novel theme and structure—this is a book about middle-aged people navigating long-term relationships, experiencing the highs and lows of love and marriage, reconciling their flaws, and making impulsive decisions that alter the course of their histories. Kundera is not a character in the book (he is all the characters!), but he is unquestionably its narrator, its Creator, and he is full of wit and wisdom and fascinating takes on all manner of things—things that, as a sophomore in college, were either outside my limited purview, way over my head, or both.

The Parmenides catalog of opposites, for example. Kundera is concerned with which, in the heavy/light polarity, is positive and which is negative. Parmenides says lightness is positive. Is it? From this recurrent discussion the title is realized:

> And Sabina—what *had* come over her? Nothing. She had left a man because she felt like leaving him. Had he persecuted her? Had he tried to take revenge on her? No. Her drama was a drama not of heaviness but of lightness. What fell to her lot was not the burden but the unbearable lightness of being.

I don't always agree with Kundera's assessment of things. In many ways he is progressive and libertine for someone born when he was, but sometimes there is an old-fashioned misogynistic view that creeps in. Take the bowler hat. He has provided us with an iconic erotic image, as I've said, but his explanation for *why* the contrast of bowler hat and lingerie is sexy is, in my opinion, wildly wrong. He argues that the hat on Sabina's head is a symbol of "violence" against her, an assault on her womanhood bordering on rape, that denies, violates, and ridicules her femininity. And, like, that's not it at all! The long-out-of-style men's hat is sexy when worn by Sabina, I believe, because, despite being a "hard masculine" object, the bowler *fails to contain her sex appeal*. It's like trying to stop a locomotive with some patriotic bunting. Wearing the hat is not a joke or a humiliation, as Kundera suggests; it is a symbol of the erotic *power* she exudes. It says: *See? Not even this ridiculous hat once worn by my grandfather can stem my sex appeal.* And because the bowler fails to stem the sexiness, it enhances it. At least, that's how I see it.

But the biggest takeaway, on this second read, is that these are characters living, or trying to live, under a dictatorship that is both petty and oppressive. There is a scene involving Tomas being interrogated by the secret police for something trivial and dumb that happened ages ago. That part did not stick with College Me at all. In 1992, a few years after the Velvet Revolution, tyrannical governments seemed like an artifact from the past: a hunk of chipped stone found in some boring museum, a tool used by primitive man that would never be relevant again. Prague was the first city in Continental Europe that I visited. That was in 1998, well after the American expats had discovered the place, but still in time for beer—*pivo*, the best on earth—to cost just 18 cents a half-litre. One night I bought a round for the entire bar, because I'd always wanted to do that. The bill was less than ten dollars.

In 2024, alas, petty, oppressive dictatorships are again on the rise—not just in Europe, but here, in the United States. One of the questions without an answer Kundera explores in *The Unbearable Lightness of Being* is whether it is better to flee from such odious autocracies or stay to resist them, even if that means loss of station, prison, or death. How many of us would have made the choice Alexei Navalny made, in returning to Russia? Not me, I don't think.

Reading through especially Part Six of the novel, titled "The Grand March," I found myself musing about, and gaining more insight into, MAGA—what it is, what it means, what it might have in store for us:

————

Artlessness

My friend Stephanie Koff has often said, and I agree, that the MAGA movement is characterized by its artlessness. There is a certain style, for sure. Kundera would call it "MAGA kitsch." Red hat, white shirt, red tie, blue suit, gold toilet. Ostentation of decor, and of plastic surgery. The movement is led by failed artists, people who, like Hitler, wanted to make their name in some or other art form, failed miserably, and transmuted that failure into vengefulness. For the last eight years Trump has collected these hateful, damaged misfits, the Stephen Millers of the world, and in a second term would deploy them to deleterious effect on the rest of us.

About Sabina, the painter in the bowler hat, Kundera writes:

At the time, she had thought that only in the Communist world could such musical barbarism reign supreme. Abroad, she discovered that the transformation of music into noise was a planetary process by which mankind was entering the historical phase of total ugliness. The total ugliness to come had made itself felt first as omnipresent acoustical ugliness: cars, motorcycles, electric guitars, drills, loudspeakers, sirens. The omnipresence of visual ugliness would soon follow.

————

Rallies

Still, in the Year of Our Lord 2024, MAGA zombies turn up at rallies, listening to Dear Leader ramble and rant. Here is Kundera, again writing about Sabina:

> A year or two after emigrating, she happened to be in Paris on the anniversary of the Russian invasion of her country. A protest march had been scheduled, and she felt driven to take part. Fists raised high, the young Frenchmen shouted out slogans condemning Soviet imperialism. She liked the slogans, but to her surprise she found herself unable to shout along with them. She lasted no more than a few minutes in the parade.
>
> When she told her French friends about it, they were amazed. "You mean you don't want to fight the occupation of your country?" She would have liked to tell them that behind Communism, Fascism, behind all occupations and invasions lurks a more basic, pervasive evil and that the image of that evil was a parade of people marching by with raised fists and shouting identical syllables in unison. But she knew she would never be able to make them understand. Embarrassed, she changed the subject.

————

Kitsch

Kundera devotes half a section of the novel explaining what "kitsch" really means. In short, it is an idealized fantasy world in which defecation does not exist. There is no excrement, nothing bad. Nobody poops. Shit—symbolizing the reality of life, and also therefore true creativity—is a theme in this section of the book.

> Those of us who live in a society where various political tendencies exist side by side and competing influences cancel

or limit one another can manage more or less to escape the kitsch inquisition: the individual can preserve his individuality; the artist can create unusual works. But whenever a single political movement corners power, we find ourselves in the realm of *totalitarian kitsch*.

When I say "totalitarian," what I mean is that everything that infringes on kitsch must be banished for life: every display of individualism (because a deviation from the collective is a spit in the eye of the smiling brotherhood); every doubt (because anyone who starts doubting details will end by doubting life itself); all irony (because in the realm of kitsch everything must be taken quite seriously); and the mother who abandons her family or the man who prefers men to women, thereby calling into question the holy decree "Be faithful and multiply."

In this light, we can regard the gulag as a septic tank used by totalitarian kitsch to dispose of its refuse.

And, a few paragraphs later:

In the realm of totalitarian kitsch, all questions are given in advance and preclude any questions. It follows, then, that the true opponent of totalitarian kitsch is the person who asks questions. A question is like a knife that slices through the stage backdrop and gives us a look at what lies hidden behind it. In fact, that was exactly how Sabina explained the meaning of her paintings to Tereza: on the surface, an intelligible lie; underneath, the unintelligible truth showing through.

MAGA kitsch, then, is a byproduct of the fairy tale the True Believers tell themselves: that Trump is here to save us, and to save the children; that the Deep State is against him, as well as the globalists, and George Soros, and Big Pharma, and Taylor Swift and Travis Kelce; that Joe Biden is the head of a crime family; that Trump sacrificed his wealth to give back to the people he loves so well; and so on. Once questioned, this world immediately falls apart. The avatar of MAGA kitsch is a rendering of Trump and Jesus, or Trump *as* Jesus.

And, finally...

———

Death Cult

Once again, it is Sabina who is the oracle:

> Living for Sabina meant seeing. Seeing is limited by two borders: strong light, which blinds, and total darkness. Perhaps that was what motivated Sabina's distaste for all extremism. Extremes mean borders beyond which life ends, and a passion for extremism, in art and in politics, is a veiled longing for death.

Perhaps that veiled longing for death explains the MAGA reluctance to wear masks, to get vaccinated, to ban automatic weapons, to accept the results of democratic elections.

———

Is life a one-shot-deal, a dress rehearsal that doubles as the sole performance of the play? Or does everything recur in a cycle of eternal return, the Nietzschean concept that inspired Kundera's novel? Is time linear, or is it, as *True Detective* tells us, a flat circle? Is fascist takeover thus inevitable? Is that why 2024 feels so significant historically? Does that explain our collective dread? Or can humankind evolve—break out of the cycle, the Yeatsian gyre, the swirling drain of the toilet of the totalitarian kitsch gulag?

Is unbearable lightness a good thing or a bad thing?

Although this does not answer these questions, I'll give

Kundera the last word: "[T]here is nothing heavier than compassion. Not even one's own pain weighs so heavy as the pain one feels with someone, for someone, a pain intensified by the imagination and prolonged by a hundred echoes."

The echoes may fade, but they never die.

CHAPTER 8
PARADISE LOST
AN EPIC POEM BY JOHN MILTON

March 10, 2024
Eight months before the election

———

TO GET my degree in English Literature, I had to take classes in two of the three Major Authors: Chaucer, Shakespeare, Milton. This was mandatory. During my semester "abroad" at NYU, I'd taken a class on Joyce. I argued with the department heads that this should satisfy the "Major Authors" requirement, but they were obdurate as Pharaoh: Joyce was not a Major Author, the Chaucer class was full, it was Milton or bust.

This wound up being a fortuitous thing. Milton was one of the best classes I took at Georgetown. (Shout-out to Professor Shulman!) My knowledge of the poet and his work was limited to Donald Sutherland's pot-smoking professor mocking him in *Animal House*. But John Milton is indeed a Major Author, and *Paradise Lost*—ten thousand lines of blank verse on the topic of Adam and Eve's expulsion from Eden, published in its final form in 1674, when the poet was 65 years old and totally blind(!)—is, unequivocally, one of the greatest works ever written in the English language.

For whatever reason, I felt, reading *Paradise Lost* in class, that I had some special insight into Milton's mindset. I connected to it. As a working text, we used a lovely, oversized 1993 edition edited by Roy Flannagan, a professor at Ohio University. I was convinced, and remain so, that his reading of the work is totally wrong. There are voluminous footnotes, most quite useful, but when Flannagan gets into the *interpretation* of the work, he's wildly off base. It got to where it was like reading Nabokov's *Pale Fire*, where the footnotes to the poem are deliberately off and tell their own story. (Indeed, I see now, flipping to the title page, that I have underlined Flannagan's name and written, in block letters: MORON. Harsh!)

Paradise Lost begins with Satan and his diabolical cohorts writhing in agony on a lake of fire in Hell, lamenting their loss to God and the army of angels. Thus the devils, by their banishment from Heaven, are the first characters to "lose" Paradise. On the very first page of my copy of the book, 22-year-old me wrote this:

> Your reading of the poem depends entirely on your definition of "lost." Pro-God reads "lost" as in "I have lost something, now I shall find it." We read "lost" as "Satan lost to God," like a battle.

Paradise lost, like the Jets lost. But…isn't that backwards? Did not Paradise prevail? It is this inversion of polarities, the question of which side is actually good and which evil, that has me thinking about *Paradise Lost* this week, as I shall soon explain.

The first two "books" are about Satan, Beelzebub, Moloch, Belial, and the other demons (literally) picking themselves off the floor, licking their wounds, processing their defeat, and figuring out what to do next. They determine, in spirited debate, that using conventional warfare to defeat God is a non-starter. The best recourse is to take His favorite charges—Adam and Eve—and convert them to the Dark Side. The rest of the work is about that diabolical endeavor, that Luciferian op, and the poem ends with the "bless't pair" banished from Eden, mirroring the demons' own banishment from Heaven. There are riveting monologues by the major characters—including the leading man in this eternal saga, Satan—interspersed with interminable passages by a long-winded narrator with a yen for literary allusion and a penchant for poor spelling. (In Milton's defense, he *was* blind.)

Convention wisdom, and Roy Flannagan, suggests that this long epic poem about well-known Biblical figures, derived from the Book of Genesis, and involving the ultimate battle between good and evil, is about religion. To which I say: Fie! It is *not* about religion; it is about politics! *Paradise Lost* is about democracy versus monarchy!

Milton was a man of faith, for sure, but he was most of all a revolutionary—a small-r republican. He was a big Oliver Cromwell guy. He even worked in Cromwell's government. He loathed the monarchy, particularly the autocratic Charles I. Milton's first big publication was the *Areopagitica; A speech of Mr. John Milton for the Liberty of Unlicenc'd Printing, to the Parlament of England*—a polemic against press censorship and a *cri de coeur* for free speech. Charles I, of course, was tried for treason and *[checks notes]* beheaded. Milton *wrote a piece justifying the regicide*. When the Commonwealth collapsed, then, he was a man on the run.

After the Restoration, Milton had to be extremely careful in expressing his still-radical political views. So he *disguised* them, in a long poem about God and the Devil. Even the narrator of the poem—which the reading public and the royal censors would conclude was Milton's own editorial voice—is pro-God. That was done, I submit, to insulate himself from danger, and should be discounted. If hauled before some court, he could plausibly claim, "But the narrator opposes these devils! Are you saying I'm not the narrator of my own poem?" The characters, and Satan in particular, give voice to what the poet *really* believed. As readers, we are supposed to identify with, to *like*, "Heaven's fugitives."

Stripped of the religious cloaking, *Paradise Lost* becomes something closer to *Star Wars*—more Jedi than Jesus. Here is the plot: Refusing to tolerate further oppression by a petty, insecure, and seemingly immortal tyrant, a coalition of muti-neers takes arms against the overlord. The rebels lose, and are exiled to a horrible place that they nevertheless warm to and take possession of. Unable to overthrow the tyrant by force, and unwilling to try again to do so, they decide instead to show the tyrant's most faithful subjects—brainwashed members of His powerful cult of personality—that the tyrant is not what He seems. In this celestial psy-op, the mutineers are successful. The subjects awaken from their stupor and see the light—even as they, too, are exiled.

There is ample textual evidence to support my reading. Hell is a democracy; Heaven is an absolute monarchy. Here is Satan, in Book One, describing life in the clouds with God:

And what is else not to be overcome?
That glory never shall his wrath or might
Extort from me. To bow and sue for grace
With suppliant knee, and deify his power
Who, from the terror of this arm, so late
Doubted his empire—that were low indeed;
That were an ignominy and shame beneath
This downfall; since, by fate, the strength of Gods,
And this empyreal substance, cannot fail;
Since, through experience of this great event,
In arms not worse, in foresight much advanced,
We may with more successful hope resolve

To wage by force or guile eternal war,
Irreconcilable to our grand Foe,
Who now triumphs, and in th' excess of joy
Sole reigning holds **the tyranny of Heaven**.

(Note: I'm going to boldface the lines I think are the most important going forward, in case the long blocks of free verse and old-timey spelling make your eyes glaze over.)

In other words, Satan refuses to kneel before the wicked tyrant, the Almighty God. Rather, he will make peace with the fiery pit they now call home. This Satan monologue is one of the most famous passages in *Paradise Lost*:

Farewell, happy fields,
Where joy for ever dwells! Hail, horrors! hail,
Infernal world! and thou, profoundest Hell,
Receive thy new possessor—one who brings
A mind not to be changed by place or time.
The mind is its own place, and in itself
Can make a Heaven of Hell, a Hell of Heaven.
What matter where, if I be still the same,
And what I should be, all but less than he
Whom thunder hath made greater? Here at least
We shall be free; th' Almighty hath not built
Here for his envy, will not drive us hence:
Here we may reign secure; and, in my choice,
To reign is worth ambition, though in Hell:
Better to reign in Hell than serve in Heaven.

In Book Two, the demons debate. It's an open debate, unlike in despotic Heaven, where God has the final and only word. The leader of the devils is not there because of force, but because he is a true leader:

Satan exalted sat, **by merit raised**

To that bad eminence;

And he intends for Hell to be ruled by the members
equally:

Where there is, then, no good
    For which to strive, no strife can grow up there
    From faction: for none sure will claim in Hell
    Precedence; none whose portion is so small
    Of present pain that with ambitious mind
    Will covet more!

Flannagan in his ridiculous footnote explains it wrongly:
"There is no reason for political factions to grow up in Hell,
since there is no reason for any fallen angel to ask for more
prominence…than he already has. Satan is lying to the angels
while he is in the act of claiming precedence in Hell. He
speaks, after all, from a throne."

But Satan is *not* lying. "We now debate," he says to his
cohorts. "Who can advise may speak." And he means it,
because the devils all have their say. And they are *all* on
thrones, like at Olympus.

Mammon points out that, even if God accepts them back
into Heaven, Heaven sucks. It's all bowing down and kissing
the ring and singing shitty songs in the choir, and he's over
that:

Suppose he should relent
And publish grace to all, on promise made
Of new subjection; with what eyes could we
Stand in his presence humble, and receive
Strict laws imposed, to celebrate his throne
With **warbled hymns**, and to his Godhead sing
Forced hallelujahs, while he lordly sits
Our envied sovereign, and his altar breathes

Ambrosial odours and ambrosial flowers,
Our servile offerings? **This must be our task
In Heaven, this our delight. How wearisome
Eternity so spent in worship paid
To whom we hate!** Let us not then pursue,
By force impossible, by leave obtained
Unacceptable, though in Heaven, our state
Of splendid vassalage; but rather **seek
Our own good from ourselves, and from our own
Live to ourselves**, though in this vast recess,
Free and to none accountable, **preferring
Hard liberty before the easy yoke
Of servile pomp.**

Beelzebub *explicitly* calls for a popular vote:

Thrones and Imperial Powers, Offspring of Heaven,
Ethereal Virtues! or these titles now
Must we renounce, and, changing style, be called
Princes of Hell? for **so the popular vote
Inclines**—here to continue, and build up here
A growing empire;

Even the narrator concedes that "with full assent / They vote." He refers to the meeting as the "Synod of Gods" and "the Stygian Counsel." They are anti-monarchy! They are small-r republicans!

Meanwhile, in Heaven, God is just a brutal, cruel tyrant, genocidal and capricious. He is unforgiving of disloyalty. Unlike Satan, He sits "High Thron'd above all highth." He is the celestial equivalent of a fascist dictator—the sort of God today's American Christian zealots obey and admire. He flat-out says he chooses a few humans to favor and leaves others out in the cold:

Some I have chosen of peculiar grace
Elect above the rest; so is my will:
The rest shall hear me call, and oft be warnd
Thir sinful state

And anyone who crosses him is toast. Not just anyone—
innocent children too. He takes out entire families, like they
do in North Korea:

Disloyal breaks his fealtie, and sinns
Against the high Supremacie of Heav'n,
Affecting God-head, and so loosing all,
To expiate his Treason hath naught left,
But to destruction sacred and devote,
He with his whole posteritie must dye,
Dye hee or Justice must; unless for him
Som other able, and as willing, pay
The rigid satisfaction, death for death.

There are plenty of other examples of the democra-
cy/monarchy polarity at work here. God is a tyrant, and His
heir is Jesus, but the problem is that God is immortal, so what
need of heirs?

In Book Five, in what is arguably the best single line in the
entire poem, an angel talking to Adam and Eve explains what
the abusive God demands from His subjects:

Our voluntarie service He requires

In certain circles this is known as "consensual non-
consent." It is the sort of mindfuck employed by cult leaders.

In Book Six, Satan reasons with Adam and Eve, explaining
his own reasons for bailing on Heaven: the death of freedom
and of individual liberty.

At first I thought that Libertie and Heav'n
To heav'nly Soules had bin all one; but now
I see that most through sloth had rather serve,
Ministring Spirits, traind up in Feast and Song;

Even the angels concede that God hoards knowledge, denying his subjects the ability to learn, as Rafael says to the couple in Book Eight:

the rest [of knowledge]
From Man or Angel the great Architect
Did wisely **to conceal, and not divulge**
His secrets to be scann'd by them who ought
Rather admire

God is afraid that, once people realize He doesn't have a monopoly on wisdom, they will turn on Him. He loves the uneducated! By Book Nine, Eve—smarter than Adam by orders of magnitude, because of course she is—has figured this all out:

Let us not then suspect our happie State
Left so imperfet by the Maker wise,
As not secure to single or combin'd.
Fraile is our happiness, if this be so,
And *Eden* were no *Eden* thus expos'd.

Basically, Paradise is Paradise in name only—PINO. Satan explains that God has "deterrd" them from

atchieving what might leade
To happier life, knowledge of Good and Evil;
Of good, how just? of evil, if what is evil
Be real, why not known, since easier shunnd?
God therefore cannot hurt ye, and be just;

Or: if He hurts you, He cannot then claim to be morally superior. That's how abusers act! Eating the apple, and thus trespassing before God, is a symbolic gesture that renounces His tyranny, that explodes His cult:

> Not just, not God; not feard then, nor obeyd:
> Your feare it self of Death removes the feare.
> Why then was this forbid? Why but to awe,
> Why but to keep ye low and ignorant,
> His worshippers; **he knows that in the day**
> **Ye Eate thereof, your Eyes that seem so cleere,**
> **Yet are but dim, shall perfetly be then**
> **Op'nd and cleerd, and ye shall be as Gods,**
> **Knowing both Good and Evil as they know**.

Again, Eve knows the deal:

> **For us alone**
> **Was death invented?** or to us deni'd
> This intellectual food, for beasts reserv'd? …
> What fear I then, rather what know to feare
> Under this ignorance of good and Evil,
> Of God or Death, of Law or Penaltie?

This is also a callback to Book One, when one of the devils suggests that trying again to attack God might compel Him to get angry enough to kill them all dead, and death—nonexistence—is preferable to living in torment or in vassalage.

Then comes the climax, which is presented from the Godcult narrator's POV:

> she pluck'd, she eat:
> Earth felt the wound, and Nature from her seat
> Sighing through all her Works gave signs of woe,
> That all was lost.

Ah, but the poem does *not* end with abject surrender, nor of doom and gloom. Adam and Eve are in the same position as Satan and the demons in Book One: exiled from a place that is superficially lovely but oppressive and soul-destroying. Eden is guarded by "angels" with flaming swords—but the two would not go back even if the gate had no sentry:

> They looking back, all th' Eastern side beheld
> Of Paradise, so late thir happie seat,
> Wav'd over by that flaming Brand, the Gate
> With dreadful Faces throng'd and fierie Armes:
> Som natural tears they drop'd, but wip'd them soon;
> **The World was all before them**, where to choose
> Thir place of rest, and Providence thir guide:
> They hand in hand with wandring steps and slow,
> Through *Eden* took thir solitarie way.

Did they lose *Paradise*? Or did Paradise *lose*? I hold with the latter. God was unable to keep them in His cult. Adam and Eve leave with nothing, as people do when leaving cults. The reward is in their newfound perspective, the capacity for wisdom, the prospect of the hopeful unknown at their feet, and the freedom to explore it. This is preferable to a life of miserable oppression.

Why was I moved to write this piece today, more than half a life after originally having this idea and making notes and marking passages in my copy of *Paradise Lost* to support my thesis? Because I have lately seen, in the actions of the Christian nationalists—Leonard Leo, Kevin Roberts, and the other zealots behind the tyrannical Project 2025—an attempt to pervert the teachings of Jesus, to cloak despotic oppression in religious imagery: to invert, as Milton does in his epic poem, the good and the evil.

The Christian Nationalists' God is petty, insecure, cruel, authoritarian. Their God, like their favored presidential candidate, demands above all else obedience and loyalty. Their God sees only a few as "elect": Mike Johnson and his ilk, straight men, blastocysts and frozen embryos. All the others He casts out. Their God is not inclusive; their Paradise, a tyrannical state. Our side, meanwhile—we who value democracy, diversity, inclusivity, toleration, separation of church and state, sharing of resources, helping the sick and vulnerable, valuing women (go, Eve, go!), and so on—they view as Satanic, just as Milton does (albeit ironically) in *Paradise Lost*. Even their new name for us—*woke*—drips with irony, as their power depends on their followers *not* waking up to the totalitarian threat to our American way of life. They rely on *withholding knowledge*, as God withholds knowledge from Adam and Eve; hence their blistering attacks on public education. In November and beyond, we must make sure, come Hell (ha ha) or high water, that this Christian Nationalist Paradise loses.

And yes, the last two weeks have been difficult to bear with respect to the news. Trump has secured some ill-deserved victories. The Supreme Court seems hellbent on helping him. The Republicans have lined up behind him. It is tempting, in these emotional troughs, to give up. I am not immune to these feelings, not by any means.

Milton has something to say about that, too. In Book One, Satan sees his defeated angels wallowing in self-pity and rebukes them:

Awake, arise, or be for ever fallen!

Tattoo those words on my very soul.

CHAPTER 9
THE WIZARD OF OZ
A FILM BY VICTOR FLEMING

December 1, 2024
One month after the election

———

SITTING around the television Thanksgiving night, looking for something other than football to watch, we landed almost immediately on *The Wizard of Oz*. This is a movie I'd seen dozens of times, but only once or twice in adulthood, and not for many years.

There is still something magical—something wizardly, even—about being able to stream *that* film, in particular, at the push of a button. "Time was," we told our Gen Z kids, "this movie came on TV once a year, and if you missed it, you had no way of watching it again until the following November." This was met with the same patronizing looks that Hunk, Hickory, and Zeke give Dorothy at the end of the picture, when she's relating what'd happened to her in Oz. "Sure, sure. Whatever you say." (TikTok Nation can never really understand what things were like back in the Before

Times, when we had to rely on rented videocassettes and dial-up modems.)

All the Americans over the age of 50 who have not seen at least *some* of *The Wizard of Oz* can comfortably fit in the backseat of a Honda Civic; the myriad horror stories about the making of the movie are explored in painstaking detail elsewhere. So I don't have much to add to extant criticism, other than to say that it's refreshing to see a fantasy film this lush that hasn't been CGI'd to death. Sure, two cast members almost died during shooting, and a stuntwoman seriously injured her leg in a mishap involving a witch's broom, but *man* that Technicolor *pops*.

What interested me is what I might take away from the film on viewing it *now*, at age 52, in the dying days of 2024, as we await the second behind-the-curtain installation of our own resident fraud. I was also curious how *The Wizard of Oz* differed from L. Frank Baum's children's book, *The Wonderful Wizard of Oz*, on which the movie is based. So on Friday, over a plate of leftover turkey, I read what seemed to me like a blatant ripoff of Lewis Carroll: *Alice's Adventures in Wonderland* in Kansas—which is not far from what Baum intended it to be. (The "wonderful" title kind of gives it away.)

Let's start with the source material. *The Wonderful Wizard of Oz* was published in May of 1900, six months before William McKinley's re-election: the apogee of overt American Empire, and the era before federal regulations, civil rights, women's suffrage, and income taxes that MAGA wants to return to. Baum—an imaginative, theatrical guy who was heavily influenced by his mother-in-law, the great abolitionist and voting rights activist Matilda Jocelyn Gage—died in May 1919, six months after Armistice Day, 18 months before the first national election in which women could vote, and three years before Judy Garland was born in Grand Rapids,

Minnesota—a small Midwestern city where, unlike in *The Wizard of Oz*, the snow is not made of asbestos.

I remember hearing that the book was some sort of allegory of nineteenth century America, in which the Scarecrow represented farmers, the Tin Woodman factory laborers, and the Cowardly Lion William Jennings Bryan, the Democratic Party presidential nominee who lost to McKinley in 1896 and 1900. I love stuff like that! So I tracked it down. Turns out that the author of this inventive theory was a high school English teacher named Henry M. Littlefield, whose essay, "The Wizard of Oz: Parable on Populism"—which would have made a nice "Sunday Pages" back in the day—ran in *American Quarterly* in 1964. He writes:

> Dorothy's house has come down on the Wicked Witch of the East, killing her. Nature, by sheer accident, can provide benefits, for indirectly the cyclone has disposed of one of the two truly bad influences in the land of Oz. Notice that evil ruled in both the East and the West; after Dorothy's coming it rules only in the West.
>
> The Wicked Witch of the East had kept the little Munchkin people "in bondage for many years, making them slave for her night and day." (pp. 22-23). Just what this slavery entailed is not immediately clear, but Baum later gives us a specific example. The Tin Woodman, whom Dorothy meets on her way to the Emerald City, had been put under a spell by the Witch of the East. Once an independent and hard working human being, the Woodman found that each time he swung his axe it chopped off a different part of his body. Knowing no other trade he "worked harder than ever," for luckily in Oz tinsmiths can repair such things. Soon the Woodman was all tin (p. 59). In this way Eastern witchcraft dehumanized a simple laborer so that the faster and better he worked the more quickly he became a kind of

machine. Here is a Populist view of evil Eastern influences on honest labor which could hardly be more pointed.

In the book, there are not *magical ruby slippers* but *charmed silver shoes*. Littlefield attaches enormous significance to this choice. Nowadays, William Jennings Bryan is known, insofar as he's known at all, for his "Cross of Gold" speech, in which he railed against the gold standard that he believed was helping rich Eastern industrialists and hurting the yeomen of the Middle West. He was for "free silver," or "bimetallism," an expansionary monetary system that would have almost certainly caused a huge spike in the inflation rate and made the Panic of 1896 into a years-long Great Disorder of the kind that roiled the German economy in the 1920s. But I digress.

Silver, Littlefield argues, "represents a real force in a land of illusion, and neither the Cowardly Lion nor Bryan truly needs or understands its use." The gold standard is represented in the book by what Baum, who was evidently unfamiliar with the Elton John song, annoyingly refers to as "the road of yellow brick."

The ragtag crew making its way to the Emerald City Littlefield compares to "Coxey's Army of tramps and indigents, marching to ask President Cleveland for work in 1894, [who appear] no more naively innocent than this group of four characters going to see a humbug Wizard, to request favors that only the little girl among them deserves." I'm not sure anyone remembered Coxey's Army even in 1900, and that incident was long forgotten by the time the motion picture came out.

Something that happens in the book but not the movie: all visitors to the Emerald City are issued emerald glasses, which are also worn by all the inhabitants of the Oz capital. That's what makes the Emerald City green. This, I think, is the most compelling piece of Littlefield's argument:

Dorothy later discovers that the greenness of dresses and ribbons disappears on leaving, and everything becomes a bland white. Perhaps the magic of any city is thus self-imposed. But the Wizard dwells here and so the Emerald City represents the national Capitol. The Wizard, a little bumbling old man, hiding behind a façade of papier-mâché and noise, might be any president from Grant to McKinley. He comes straight from the fairgrounds of Omaha, Nebraska, and he symbolizes the American criterion for leadership—he is able to be everything to everybody.

Thus, in 1964, does Littlefield equate the Great Oz with the Chief Executive, a fraud who is, in reality, a bumbling old man. *He is able to be everything to everybody.*

Baum was not an overtly political guy, and certainly no kind of activist. Whether he intended *The Wonderful Wizard of Oz* to be a veiled commentary of the turn-of-the-century United States—whether he was himself the political pundit behind the curtain—is anybody's guess. Even so, Littlefield's theory is compelling. The geopolitics of Oz support his argument. The North and the South are presided over by "good" witches; the West and the East, by "wicked" ones. Consider: an American writer who was born in Union territory four years before the Civil War would probably be more inclined to install a wicked witch in the *South,* not the East.

By the time the movie came out, all of that gold standard stuff was ancient history. The winds of change were blowing hard enough to uproot Dorothy's house and hurl it over the rainbow. The U.S. was suffering through the tenth(!) year of a crippling depression that seemed endless. In Europe, fascism was on the march: in Italy, in Spain, in Germany. *The Wizard of Oz* was released nationwide on August 25, 1939—exactly one week before Adolf Hitler's Nazis rolled into Poland, kicking off the Second World War.

And so, as the world teetered on the brink of fascist hegemony, Hollywood was concocting, and moviegoers were thirsty for, fantastical landscapes populated by Flying Monkeys, members in good standing of the Lollipop Guild, angry apple trees, and lions who talk like Edward G. Robinson. Not that I blame them. Who among us wouldn't want to vanish over the rainbow sometime between now and January 20th?

Here are some observations from Thursday's viewing:

First, this is a movie dominated by strong women. In Oz, the patriarchy has been smashed! With the exception of the eponymous wizard—who turns out to be a total grifter—all of the power is concentrated in the hands of women. The men of the movie, meanwhile, are cowards and frauds. Dorothy is the unquestioned leader of her group of misfits; the Wicked Witch of the West is the formidable villain; Glinda, the "good" witch, who is actually kind of an asshole, ultimately reveals the secret to getting back to Kansas. And back in Kansas, Auntie Em oversees the farmhands with an iron fist; she takes on the malevolent Miss Gulch, while Uncle Henry grins idiotically, and perhaps drunkenly, in his well-worn chair.

And then there is the conflict that initiates the film's action. The aforementioned Almira Gulch—who, we're told, owns half the county—shows up on her bicycle with an order from the sheriff: Toto, Dorothy's beloved dog, who has growled and snapped at the mean old lady, is to be seized by Gulch and taken to be "destroyed." Em gives her a piece of her mind, sort of, but ultimately yields. "We can't go against the law," she explains to Dorothy. Gulch takes Toto and puts him in a picnic basket, from which the clever pooch promptly escapes. He returns home, whereupon Dorothy decides to run away, for Toto's protection.

None of that is in the book. Almira Gulch is exclusively a cinematic invention.

And while that scene is textbook Hollywood emotional manipulation—What child watching *The Wizard of Oz* wants to see Toto euthanized? Who blames Dorothy for getting the hell out of there?—it does not seem far-fetched to suggest that a sequence from a 1939 movie involving a heartless agent of the state coming to collect the most vulnerable member of a household, with the full backing of the law, and for the express purpose of extermination, was, consciously or otherwise, written with Nazis in mind. Art imitates life.

But the most ominous takeaway from watching *The Wizard of Oz* in 2024 is this: even as THE END appears on the sepia screen, *the initial conflict remains unresolved*. At the denouement, Dorothy is back in her bed, surrounded by all of her loved ones: Auntie Em and Uncle Henry; Zeke, Hickory, and Hunk. Even Professor Marvel takes a break from advising the Crowned Heads of Europe to check in on her. At some point, we *should* learn that Almira Gulch died in the cyclone—that a house really did fall on her—but no! Dorothy is so relieved to be home, so happy to be back with her dour aunt and useless uncle, that the grim reality of her situation seems to have eluded her: *Toto's escape is temporary*, and no amount of water will deter the oligarchical Miss Gulch from returning to claim the dog.

"There's no place like home," while an objectively true statement, is, on its face, neither positive nor negative. Home could be good; home could be bad; we don't know. The movie asks us to think of "home" as a magical place, even as Dorothy spends most of her screen-time exploring a place that is *literally* magical. Even as a child, I wondered why she would want to return to bleak, lonely Kansas, when she could stay in Oz with her colorful new friends.

Once landed over the rainbow, Dorothy goes to great lengths to make it back home, only to find that home is just as unsafe as it had been when she decided to leave it. Home is where "ding dong" means that the witch is not dead but at the door, basket at the ready, eager to go full Kristi Noem on Toto. We are back where we started. Nothing has changed.

The ending of *The Wizard of Oz*, then, is ambiguous. The lost child is returned, and the thankful adults are gathered round her bed, in a formation of protection—swell. But what will the grown-ups do when the Nazi returns? Will they capitulate, like Auntie Em did the first time? Or, given a second chance, will they fight back? We are not told.

Fifty days from today, our own Almira Gulch / humbug Oz / overgrown orange Munchkin will return to power. Fifty days from today, Donald Trump (his name even *sounds* like something Frank Baum cooked up!) will retake the White House—which, even with the increase in cyclones due to climate change, is unlikely to rise into the D.C. air and fall on top of the Wicked Witch of the East Side.

The danger is real, is imminent. Goodbye, Yellow Brick Road; hello, red MAGA hat.

Given a second chance, what will *we* do?

CHAPTER 10
BLEAK HOUSE

A NOVEL BY CHARLES DICKENS

December 22, 2024
One month before inauguration

———

IF CHARLES DICKENS were alive today, and at the peak of his considerable powers, he would not invest his energies writing interminable novels for an increasingly book-averse population. Instead of waiting for fresh serialized chapters of *David Copperfield*, we'd be eagerly anticipating the next episode of a series of that title to drop on HBO. Twenty twenty-four Dickens would be Shonda Rhimes—creative dynamo, showrunner of some of the most popular, most watched, and most lucrative programs on television, with a thousand projects big and small going at all once.

Commercially- and critically-successful creative dynamo is what Dickens was in his own period, which is to say the era between the publication of the first installment of *The Pickwick Papers* in April 1836—a year before Queen Victoria took the throne—to the scrawling of the last lines of the unfinished *Mystery of Edwin Drood*, as he lay dying, at age 58, in

June 1870. Unlike many writers, who are given to shyness, he was an enormous personality in real life. He was a gifted mimic, a talented comic performer with great stage presence, and he may well have gone into his beloved theater if the chips had fallen differently. He wrote voluminous correspondence and took in plays and did some acting and directing and wrote letters to newspapers and contributed some journalism and went on speaking tours and traveled around Europe and the United States, and he walked a dozen miles a day around London, and he fathered ten children, and he spent the last dozen years of his life living "in sin" with a woman who nowadays would be his second wife but back then was a secret partner because the discovery of their forbidden relationship would have been scandalous, and while he was doing all of THAT, this literary Energizer Bunny was banging out novel after novel after novel, bestseller after bestseller after bestseller, each one longer than the next. *Bleak House*, which some consider his best literary work, checks in at over 358,000 words!

I have long resisted Dickens. He got paid by the word, and was thus financially incentivized to add extra padding to the books; this always struck me as too commercial an approach to produce great literary fiction. And the character names, while delightful—Ebenezer Scrooge, of course; but also Oliver Twist, Martin Chuzzlewit, Uriah Heep, Sophy Wackles, Lucretia Tox, Charity Pecksniff, and *[checks notes]* Dick Swiveller—are too silly to be taken seriously. Any of the appellations just listed could plausibly be the stage name of some lesser porn star.

(It is a fun game to pick which figures in the MAGA universe have Dickens names. Elon Musk, most definitely. Hope Hicks, for sure. Seb Gorka, Mehmet Oz, Mike and Sarah Huckabee. Marsha Blackburn could have been a minor character who spontaneously combusts, as Krook does in *Bleak House*. And with his Dickensian name, his caricature of a personality, his naked parsimony, and his active malevolence, especially towards children, Donald Trump might just as well be a character in the novel. We can easily imagine him surveying the Bleak House grounds and remarking on what a fine golf course he could make of it.)*

In high school, I read *Great Expectations*. I've tried several times since to re-read it, but I can't get past the child abuse depicted in the first chapters. As good as the introduction to *A Tale of Two Cities* is—although often misconstrued†—I lose the plot by chapter three. And I've seen a thousand variations of *A Christmas Carol* but never delved in to the original text. That's the full extent of my Dickens reading.

But then, a few weeks ago, the thick Penguin Classics paperback of *Bleak House*, which has been in my possession for God knows how long, called out to me, for three days in a row, from its place on the dusty shelves. With my brain feeling like an old car that just hit 200,000 miles, I knew it would do me some good to read, and not just read but *finish*, a long novel. Long-novel-reading is like Pilates for the mind —it exercises muscles not much used in quotidian life, and that are otherwise in danger of atrophying. It was time, I decided, to get my Dickens on. And so, over the course of a

---

* Bleak House is the name of John Jarndyce's estate, where the three teenagers, wards of Chancery, go to live at the opening of the novel. The name is ironical. The place is anything but bleak, and made all the less so by the welcome infusion of youth and hope and beauty. The actual house of bleakness that the title refers to, rather, is the home of Sir Leicester Dedlock, Baronet, and Lady Dedlock, who is, Dickens tells us, "bored to death."

† The most famous line from Dickens, I think, is the opening of *A Tale of Two Cities*: "It was the best of times, it was the worst of times." I always took that to mean a sense of equilibrium, a balancing of the scales; or, perhaps, that the era could be good or bad depending on one's perspective. But what he really means is that the late 18th century, when that book is set, is an Age of Extremes. He's saying: "Oh my God, this is the greatest, biggest, greatest year there ever was" and also, "Good Lord, this is the shittiest, worst, vilest 12 months of all time ever." Might 2025 be like that?

few weeks, I made my slow, steady way through all 989 pages.

In his lecture on *Bleak House*, first given while teaching at Wellesley College in 1941,* Vladimir Nabokov said that to tackle the novel, "We just surrender ourselves to Dickens's voice—that is all. . . All we have to do when reading *Bleak House* is relax and let our spines take over. Although we read with our minds, the seat of artistic delight is between the shoulder blades. That little shiver behind is quite certainly the highest form of emotion that humanity has attained when evolving pure art and pure science...The brain only continues the spine: the wick goes through the whole candle. If we are not capable of enjoying that shiver, if we cannot enjoy literature, then let us give up the whole thing and concentrate on our comics, our videos, our books-of-the-week." (If updated for today, he might have instead said, "our TikToks, our Instagram reels, our Netflix specials, our Spotify wraps.")

"But," he continues, "I think Dickens will prove stronger." One of my favorite writers, Nabokov has provided my spine with no short supply of shivers. So if *he* says we should surrender to Dickens's voice, and that said voice is powerful enough to drown out the noise around us, well, that's good enough for me.

Lo, Nabokov was right. Dickens is—here's a hot take—a magnificent writer in terms of the construction of sentences, the vast vocabulary at his disposal, the wry deployment of jokes, the poetry of individual paragraphs, and the weaving together of seemingly endless strands of plot-lines, transforming, with almost architectural precision, what seems like a mountainous pile of clumped-together yarn (like the one in our bedroom that my wife, as I type this, is endeavoring to

---

* The consummate writer, Nabokov wrote all his lectures down. The *Bleak House* lecture is included in *Lectures on Literature*, published posthumously in 1980.

untangle) into a perfectly knit work of art. As Nabokov puts it, "The magic trick Dickens is out to perform implies balancing these three globes [i.e., the three themes of the book], juggling with them, keeping them in a state of coherent unity, maintaining these three balloons in the air without getting their strings snarled."

And, yes: Dickens brings the spine-shivers. Making my way through the book, I stopped countless times to admire a passage. Here is one paragraph, well into a very long book, right after the disappearance of the wonderfully named Lady Dedlock—lovely in its construction, gorgeous in its word choices, and poetical in its observations:

> As all partings foreshadow the great final one, so, empty rooms, bereft of a familiar presence, mournfully whisper what your room and what mine must one day be. My Lady's state has a hollow look, thus gloomy and abandoned; and in the inner apartment, where [the detective] Mr. Bucket last night made his secret perquisition, the traces of her dresses and her ornaments, even the mirrors accustomed to reflect them when they were a portion of herself, have a desolate and vacant air. Dark and cold as the wintry day is, it is darker and colder in these deserted chambers than in many a hut that will barely exclude the weather; and though the servants heap fires in the grates and set the couches and the chairs within the warm glass screens that let their ruddy light shoot through to the furthest corners, there is a heavy cloud upon the rooms which no light will dispel.

And here we have a perfect example of a typical Dickensian paragraph, piled high, like a fancy sandwich at some renowned Philadelphia deli, with all the key ingredients of his best work: long, billowy sentences; repetition of words and phrases; lists; granular familiarity with London, and with its inhabitants high and low (with more sympathy, always, for the latter); and, to prove the point, a not-so-subtle jab at the rich and powerful, served up in a flowery piece of writing which elegance belies its implicit disgust. Mr. Bucket, mentioned here, is a police inspector:

Wintry morning, looking with dull eyes and sallow face upon the neighborhood of Leicester Square, finds its inhabitants unwilling to get out of bed. Many of them are not early risers at the brightest of times, being birds of night who roost when the sun is high and are wide awake and keen for prey when the stars shine out. Behind dingy blind and curtain, in upper story and garret, skulking more or less under false names, false hair, false titles, false jewelry, and false histories, a colony of brigands lie in their first sleep. Gentlemen of the green-baize road who could discourse from personal experience of foreign galleys and home treadmills; spies of strong governments that eternally quake with weakness and miserable fear, broken traitors, cowards, bullies, gamesters, shufflers, swindlers, and false witnesses; some not unmarked by the branding-iron beneath their dirty braid; all with more cruelty in them than was in Nero, and more crime than is in Newgate. For howsoever bad the devil can be in fustian or smock-frock (and he can be very bad in both), he is a more designing, callous, and intolerable devil when he sticks a pin in his shirt-front, calls himself a gentleman, backs a card or color, plays a game or so of billiards, and knows a little about bills and promissory notes, than in any other form he wears. And in such form Mr. Bucket shall find him, when he will, still pervading the tributary channels of Leicester Square.

And here is another shorter but no less exquisite passage deep in the novel, concerning Sir Leicester Dedlock's powerful and mysterious attorney, one Mr. Tulkinghorn:

The time was once when men as knowing as Mr. Tulking-horn would walk on turret-tops in the starlight and look up into the sky to read their fortunes there. Hosts of stars are visible to-night, though their brilliancy is eclipsed by the splendor of the moon. If he be seeking his own star as he methodically turns and turns upon the leads, it should be but a pale one to be so rustily represented below. If he be tracing out his destiny, that may be written in other characters nearer to his hand.

Mr. Tulkinghorn does not make many appearances in the novel's 67 chapters, but when he does materialize, with his grim gravitas, unknowable poker face, and ill intent, we know, as readers, to stand up straight and pay attention, as if he were an actual attorney, funded by rich and villainous Republicans, come to take our deposition, on which our family's future depends.

There's a lot going on in *Bleak House*, but ultimately, the book is a scathing commentary on lawyers—a profession which, as a whole, Mr. Dickens is not particularly fond of. Rather, he seems to hold with Mr. George, the military veteran and gun-shop owner, accused, falsely, of a homicide:

> "You won't have a lawyer?"
> "No, sir." Mr. George shook his head in the most
> emphatic manner. "I thank you all the same, sir, but—
> no lawyer!"
> "Why not?"
> "I don't take kindly to the breed," said Mr. George.

And since the homicide in question is Mr. Tulkinghorn's, the "whodunit" narrative that dominates the last third of the novel quite literally involves an eminently capable investigator, said Mr. Bucket, trying to determine which, among the many, many primary, secondary and tertiary characters that might have wanted the terrifying lawyer dead, actually did the deed.

Dickens doesn't hide his disdain for the Chancery Court—that is, the court that deals with wills, probates, estates, and other civil matters.* He lets us know his feelings right up front, in the fifth and sixth paragraphs of the first chapter:

> Never can there come fog too thick, never can there come mud and mire too deep, to assort with the groping and floundering condition which this High Court of Chancery, most pestilent of hoary sinners, holds this day in the sight of heaven and earth.
>
> On such an afternoon, if ever, the Lord High Chancellor ought to be sitting here—as here he is—with a foggy glory round his head, softly fenced in with crimson cloth and curtains, addressed by a large advocate with great whiskers, a little voice, and an interminable brief, and outwardly directing his contemplation to the lantern in the roof, where he can see nothing but fog. On such an afternoon some score of members of the High Court of Chancery bar ought to be—as here they are—mistily engaged in one of the ten thousand stages of an endless cause, tripping one another up on slippery precedents, groping knee-deep in technicalities, running their goat-hair and horsehair warded heads against walls of words and making a pretence of equity with serious faces, as players might. On such an afternoon the various solicitors in the cause, some two or three of whom have inherited it from their fathers, who made a fortune by it, ought to be—as are they not?—ranged in a line, in a long matted well (but you might look in vain for truth at the bottom of it) between the registrar's red table and the silk gowns, with bills, cross-bills,

---

* In 1852-3, when *Bleak House* was published, the Chancery was notorious for being slow, bewildering, and unfair; the book helped bring about much needed court reform.

answers, rejoinders, injunctions, affidavits, issues, references to masters, masters' reports, mountains of costly nonsense, piled before them. Well may the court be dim, with wasting candles here and there; well may the fog hang heavy in it, as if it would never get out; well may the stained-glass windows lose their color and admit no light of day into the place; well may the uninitiated from the streets, who peep in through the glass panes in the door, be deterred from entrance by its owlish aspect and by the drawl, languidly echoing to the roof from the padded dais where the Lord High Chancellor looks into the lantern that has no light in it and where the attendant wigs are all stuck in a fog-bank! This is the Court of Chancery, which has its decaying houses and its blighted lands in every shire, which has its worn-out lunatic in every madhouse and its dead in every churchyard, which has its ruined suitor with his slipshod heels and threadbare dress borrowing and begging through the round of every man's acquaintance, which gives to monied might the means abundantly of wearying out the right, which so exhausts finances, patience, courage, hope, so overthrows the brain and breaks the heart, that there is not an honourable man among its practitioners who would not give—who does not often give—the warning, "Suffer any wrong that can be done you rather than come here!"

The book's "MacGuffin" is an eternal probate case, *Jarndyce and Jarndyce*, which has been wending its way through the Chancery Court, seemingly from time immemorial. The main characters are all connected to the case or the Court. Some are extended members of the Jarndyce family, on one side or the other of the internecine legal battle. Some, like the aforementioned Mr. Tulkinghorn, are lawyers. Others earn their daily bread by doing business with and for the Court and its lawyers, while still more have some tangential connection to the Court, the case, or the other characters. The molassesine morass of the Chancery Court and the self-serving avarice of everyone involved with *Jarndyce and Jarndyce*, legal professionals and suitors both, are at the heart of *Bleak House*.

Perhaps this is what drew me to this novel at this time—our current legal profession's contemptible deployment of lawfare to silence dissent. This week, Trump filed a lawsuit against the *Des Moines Register* and an individual pollster, Ann Seltzer, for *running a poll* suggesting—wrongly as it turned out, to our great dismay—that he was losing in Iowa. This, Trump's ridiculous lawsuit claimed, amounted to "brazen election interference." He will lose this case, but that's not the point. The point is to sap his critics of time, money, energy, and the will to live. That new lawsuit came on the heels of a speedy settlement Donald arrived at with ABC News, which corporate overlords, despite their deep pockets, pusillanimously decided not to fight for the First Amendment in court.

The vengeful President-Elect is not the only MAGA figure to file frivolous lawsuits with the aim of thwarting and/or silencing critics. Devin Nunes sued a pseudonymous Twitter user, Devin's Cow. Elon Musk sued Media Matters. Mike Flynn sued the indefatigable Jim Stewartson and the Lincoln Project's Rick Wilson. That last case was tossed out earlier this month.

"If the purpose of terror is to terrorize," Wilson wrote of his unpleasant and expensive experience, "the purpose of lawfare is also to terrorize. The tools and techniques of lawfare, particularly these loonbucket defamation suits, would terrify people without means, experience, and strong legal representation."

If the Trump people keep up with this "SLAPP" lawsuits —and, being soulless ghouls, they will—perhaps the Amer-ican Bar Association, or the bars of the individual states, might take some decisive action and start eighty-six ing the attorneys who are serial participants in this systematic legal harassment. But I won't hold my breath.

Deep into the novel, in a chapter devoted to another amoral attorney, the gray and dull Mr. Vholes, Dickens gives us as unvarnished an assessment as can be found in the thousand pages:

> The one great principle of the English law is to make business for itself. There is no other principle distinctly, certainly, and consistently maintained through all its narrow turnings. Viewed by this light it becomes a coherent scheme and not the monstrous maze the laity are apt to think it. Let them but once clearly perceive that its grand principle is to make business for itself at their expense, and surely they will cease to grumble.

> But not perceiving this quite plainly—only seeing it by halves in a confused way—the laity sometimes suffer in peace and pocket, with a bad grace, and DO grumble very much.

What was true of English law then is, if I might suggest, equally true of U.S. law today. Furthermore, we might also, at the butt-end of the Year of our Lord 2024, replace, in that wonderfully candid passage, "the English law" with "the American legacy media," "the American political system," "the American entertainment industry," and, as a nod to the contemporary assassin with the Dickensian monicker of Luigi Mangione, "the American for-profit healthcare industry."

Money makes the world go round, and their side has a lot more of it than ours—or, at least, a lot more that they are willing to blow on assholery of the kind that will chill journalism and hasten our descent into dictatorship. Democracy doesn't die in darkness; democracy dies in deposition.

There is also Trump's fascination with the Gilded Age, the Robber Baron era. Dickens was dead a quarter century before

McKinley was elected in 1894, and his descriptions of London are largely drawn from his own childhood in the 1820s. Even so, we can see in *Bleak House* the qualities that, to Donald's way of thinking, are what made America so great back in the 1890s: child labor, unsafe housing, air and water pollution, outbreaks of diseases we now vaccinate against, domestic violence, rigid class systems, women as second-class citizens, and, of course, the existence of monarchs.

What I like most about Dickens is that he addresses grim subjects without being a total downer—and thus avoids making us want to stop reading. There is always a level of detachment from the goings-on. Not that we are not emotionally connected—I loved Lady Dedlock, and Esther Summerson, and John Jarndyce—but we never quite feel the danger ourselves. We readers are in a safe space, protected like Mr. Jarndyce protects Miss Summerson.

Dickens is never not optimistic. For all the death and shame and bankruptcy and contagion and dirt and fog and smoke and fire, for all the corrupt lawyers and nasty blackmailers and abused children and homicidal housekeepers, *Bleak House* is ultimately a hopeful book. If we are shown the worst of humanity, we are also given examples of people at their best—paragons of virtue and decency.

In the 67th and final chapter of the book, the exemplary Esther, our occasional narrator, describes her happiness with her marriage to Allan Woodcourt, a small-town doctor who is the love of her life:

> We are not rich in the bank, but we have always prospered, and we have quite enough. I never walk out with my husband but I hear the people bless him. I never go into a house of any degree but I hear his praises or see them in grateful eyes. I never lie down at night but I know that in the course of that day he has alleviated pain and soothed some fellow-creature in the time of need. I know that from the beds

of those who were past recovery, thanks have often, often gone up, in the last hour, for his patient ministration. Is not this to be rich?

It is, Esther. It is indeed.

And some of us don't even require a visit from the Ghost of Christmas Future to know it.

CHAPTER 11

THE BIG SLEEP

A NOVEL BY RAYMOND
CHANDLER

December 29, 2024
Three weeks before inauguration

———

IF WE KNEW nothing about Raymond Chandler, the
author of American detective fiction *ne plus ultra*, we might
reasonably assume that he grew up in Los Angeles and
watched the city change with the advent of the motion
picture; that he once worked as a policeman or a detective
himself, as the spy novelists Graham Greene, Ian Fleming,
and John Le Carré all spent time with the British intelligence
services; that he ran liquor during Prohibition; and that the
"common" patois spoken by his characters, the colorful
language of the street, was picked up from intimate familiarity with various and sundry degenerates.

None of those things are even close to being true.

Born in 1888 in Chicago, Chandler almost immediately
moved to Plattsmouth, Nebraska, south of Omaha on the
Missouri—and after his father, a feckless drunk, ran off, relo-
cated with his Irish-born mother to the south of London. He

spent his formative years in England and became a British citizen. Listening to the hard-boiled American badinage in his work, one would never guess that he was a graduate of Dulwich College, a well-regarded public school (in the British sense) that also produced P.G. Wodehouse and C.S. Forester. He didn't even show up in L.A. until 1913—just in time for the 25-year-old to go fight with the Canadian Expeditionary Force in the Great War.

Upon his return to Los Angeles in 1918, Chandler began a relationship with Pearl "Cissy" Pascal. The pairing was unlikely to last because Cissy was 1) married, 2) stepmother to an army friend of Raymond's, 3) disapproved of by his mother, and 4) eighteen years older. But the two were together until her death in 1954, an event Chandler mourned so passionately that he attempted suicide soon after.

Not that it was a perfect union. He would have affairs with many of the women in his life: his agent, his secretaries, wives and widows of writer friends. And like his father, he was an alcoholic. The mixing of business and pleasure and a tendency to drink on the job are attributes Chandler bequeathed to his greatest literary creation, the private detective Philip Marlowe, and suit that sleuth as well as they do another womanizing lush of midcentury fiction, James Bond —but they did not serve Chandler well in real life. At his fancy job working for an oil concern in the 1920s, he was an HR nightmare (or would have been, had their been HR departments before the New Deal), and his drinking and philandering eventually led to the termination of his employment.

Only when he was let go in 1931 did Chandler embark upon the literary career he'd been quietly nurturing since boyhood. When his first novel, *The Big Sleep*, was published in 1939, he was 51 years old—just a year younger than I am right now, and twice as old as many if not most debut novelists.

His behavior towards the women in his life informs the

casual misogyny that permeates his work: "The Big Seep," as the noir novelist Megan Abbott smartly phrases it, in her fantastic 2018 essay on the subject. It must be reckoned with.

"What fascinates and compels me most about Chandler in this #MeToo moment are the ways his novels speak to our current climate," Abbott writes. "Because if you want to understand toxic white masculinity, you could learn a lot by looking at noir."

She continues:

> Loosely defined, *noir* describes the flood of dark, fatalistic books and films that emerged before, during, and especially after World War II. As scholars like Janey Place have pointed out, this was an era when many white American men felt embattled. Their livelihoods had been taken away—first by the Depression, then by the war, and then by the women who replaced them while they were off fighting. Into this climate noir flowered: Tales of white, straight men—the detective, the cop, the sap—who feel toppled from their rightful seat of power and who feel deeply threatened by women, so threatened that they render them all-powerful and blame them for all the bad things these straight white men do. Kill a guy, rob a bank—the femme fatale made me do it. These novels simmer with resentment over perceived encroachment and a desire to contain female power.

Depression-era detectives, real and imagined, were not "woke," and expecting—or, worse, demanding—that they retroactively adopt modern standards of acceptable male behavior (that, incidentally, too many men in 2024 have yet to adopt) is both ridiculous and boring. Plus, as Abbott says, we can learn from it.

Reading *The Big Sleep*, which is narrated by Marlowe—just as Conrad's *Heart of Darkness* is narrated by Marlow—I see an honorable but lonely man struggling to explicate human nature. He wants to break everything down to the tiniest detail but can't. He errs on the side of distrust. He dons emotional armor to steel himself against the female charms he's otherwise susceptible to. He is a straight white man who abides by a rigid moral code developed by straight white men, and anyone who isn't a straight white man simultaneously fascinates and befuddles, attracts and repulses him. He is more sensitive than he lets on; I would characterize Marlowe's masculinity as more bewildered than toxic.

So, yes: there is much to learn, good and bad, about men, and manhood, and masculinity, from these pages.

———

In person, Chandler was funny, clever, well-acquainted with people of all manner of backgrounds, and highly observant. He was also clinically depressed, painfully judgmental, deeply insecure, and cynical as hell. One can be highly observant without being cynical, but one cannot be cynical without being highly observant. As Ambrose Bierce quipped, the cynic is "a blackguard whose faulty vision sees things as they are, not as they ought to be."

Chandler might call this realism. In his 1950 essay, "The Simple Art of Murder," a discourse on detective fiction that is the introduction to an anthology of his short stories, he writes:

> The realist in murder writes of a world in which gangsters can rule nations and almost rule cities, in which hotels and apartment houses and celebrated restaurants are owned by men who made their money out of brothels, in which a screen star can be the finger man for a mob, and the nice man down the hall is a boss of the numbers racket; a world where a judge with a cellar full of bootleg liquor can send a man to jail for having a pint in his pocket, where the mayor of your

town may have condoned murder as an instrument of money-making, where no man can walk down a dark street in safety because law and order are things we talk about but refrain from practicing; a world where you may witness a hold-up in broad daylight and see who did it, but you will fade quickly back into the crowd rather than tell any one, because the hold-up men may have friends with long guns, or the police may not like your testimony, and in any case the shyster for the defense will be allowed to abuse and vilify you in open court, before a jury of selected morons, without any but the most perfunctory interference from a political judge.

A little too on the nose, right? That paragraph was written three quarters of a century ago, but in it, we glimpse Vladimir Putin, and Donald Trump, and Matt Gaetz, and Clarence Thomas, and Rudy Giuliani, and any one of a thousand witnesses to the crimes of Jeffrey Epstein and Sean Combs. Does that say something about all men? About human nature in general? Or it is a strictly American phenomenon? Captain Gregory, the head of the Missing Persons Department in *The Big Sleep*, makes no bones about it, telling Marlowe:

Being a copper I like to see the law win. I'd like to see the flashy well-dressed muggs like [mobster] Eddie Mars spoiling their manicures in the rock quarry at Folsom, alongside of the poor little slumbred hard guys that got knocked over on their first caper and never had a break since. That's what I'd like. You and me both lived too long to think I'm likely to see it happen. Not in this town, not in any town half this size, in any part of this wide, green and beautiful U.S.A. We just don't run our country that way.

We didn't run the country that way in 1939, we don't run

it that way in 2024, and 2025 looks like it will be a banner year for flashy well-dressed muggs.

"It is not a fragrant world," Chandler says in his essay, "but it is the world you live in."

———

Few writers wrote about our unfragrant world as giftedly as Raymond Thornton Chandler. There is some Hemingway in his voice, and some Hammett in his sensibilities, but no one is quite like him. On almost every page of *The Big Sleep*, there is some poetical passage or paragraph, a clever witticism or creative metaphor: the sort of top-drawer prose not usually given to detective fiction, that leaps out from the page.

This is a throwaway line that Chandler makes beautiful:

Under the thinning fog the surf curled and creamed, almost without sound, like a thought trying to form itself on the edge of consciousness.

The second time Marlowe encounters the troubled Carmen Sternwood, at what winds up being a murder scene, he reports:

She was wearing a pair of long jade earrings. They were nice earrings and had probably cost a couple of hundred dollars. She wasn't wearing anything else.

Finally, there is this beauty, which is engraved on his tombstone:

Dead men are heavier than broken hearts.

———

Here is the opening paragraph of *The Big Sleep*:

> It was about eleven o'clock in the morning, mid October, with the sun not shining and a look of hard wet rain in the clearness of the foothills. I was wearing my powder-blue suit, with dark blue shirt, tie and display handkerchief, black brogues, black wool socks with dark blue clocks on them. I was neat, clean, shaved and sober, and I didn't care who knew it. I was everything the well-dressed private detective ought to be. I was calling on four million dollars.

Note how much information is conveyed in those five sentences: We know the time of day, the season, the weather, and the forecast. We have a sense of the terrain. We know what he's wearing—everything dark, everything black (although blue and black, my mother always said, do not match), but patterned socks that suggest he doesn't take himself too seriously. We know from his decision to include "sober" among the four adjectives to describe himself that there are plenty of occasions when he is anything but that. We know he's ashamed of his drinking. We know his profession. We know he has a keen eye for detail. We know he works alone. And we know he's a fish out of water—dressed to meet someone with old money the way he thinks someone with old money would want him to dress. Four million dollars in 1939 is equivalent to $90 million today.

In the second paragraph, Chandler reveals the theme of the novel and hints at the plot—although we don't know it yet. He's thrown a fastball right over the plate, and we just let it go by:

> The main hallway of the Sternwood place was two stories high. Over the entrance doors, which would have led in a troop of Indian elephants, there was a broad stained glass panel showing a knight in dark armor rescuing a lady who

was tied to a tree and didn't have any clothes on but some very long and convenient hair. The knight had pushed the visor of his helmet back to be sociable, and he was fiddling with the knots on the ropes that tied the lady to the tree and not getting anywhere. I stood there and thought that if I lived in the house, I would sooner or later have to climb up there and help him. He didn't really seem to be trying.

What Marlowe will do, over the course of the novel's 231 pages, is, basically, insert himself into the stained glass panel to help rescue the lady. The noir detective, after all, is just a modern twist on the white knight archetype from the age of chivalry, going off on perilous adventures at the behest of his lady. He's not in it for sex. He's not in it for money, not really. He's in it to restore balance, to right the wrongs. He's in it for honor.

"Marlowe is nearly celibate, avoids carrying a gun, and only shoots a man once," Abbott points out. "His isolation from others is profound. Forever unattached and seemingly friendless, he feels increasingly out of place in a changing Los Angeles." He *is* the knight in the stained glass panel.

Chandler was well aware of the kind of character he sought to create in Philip Marlowe. It's all very intentional. The guy's allusive last name, after all, is the same as that of an Elizabethan playwright, much celebrated at Dulwich College, who was no stranger to the seedy side of life. In "The Simple Art of Murder," he details who exactly the noir detective must be:

> In everything that can be called art there is a quality of redemption. . . [D]own these mean streets a man must go who is not himself mean, who is neither tarnished nor afraid. The detective in this kind of story must be such a man. He is the hero; he is everything.
>
> He is a relatively poor man, or he would not be a detec-

tive at all. He is a common man or he would not go among
common people. He has a sense of character, or he would not
know his job. He will take no man's money dishonestly and
no man's insolence without a due and dispassionate revenge.
He is a lonely man and his pride is that you will treat him as
a proud man or be very sorry you ever saw him. He talks as
the man of his age talks—that is, with with rude wit, a lively
sense of the grotesque, a disgust for sham, and a contempt
for pettiness.

The story is this man's adventure in search of a hidden
truth, and it would be no adventure if it did not happen to a
man fit for adventure.

Megan Abbott says she is drawn to Chandler "because the
world he brings to life so vividly is a world I understand,
especially now. It's a world of peril, a troubled and troubling
place where it feels harder and harder to make things right."

That was true in 2018, and even more so now. In a world
of crooked politicians, corrupt judges, captured corporate
media, cowardly attorneys general, and capitulation all
around; an artless world, out of balance and off kilter, that
seems increasingly divorced from reality; a world that
elevates the simple and the stupid, the profane and the profi-
teering, the inhuman and the inhumane—in this world, we
need someone unafraid to speak truth to power, to hold the
bad guys accountable, to make things right, to jump headlong
into the stained glass window and free us from our bondage.
To save the day.

Do Philip Marlowes only exist in works of fiction? And if
so, does the fact that our alternative-truth reality has *become* a
work of fiction mean that a hero will one day emerge, and put
things right, and rescue us from the bad guys, for $25 a day
plus expenses?

The evidence suggests otherwise. Jim Comey was not that
person. Neither was Robert Mueller, or Christopher Wray, or

Merrick Garland, or even Jack Smith—although he came the closest. And yet we ache for this salvation. We yearn for justice. We are so desperate for these Marlovian qualities that we have collectively projected them upon a cold-blooded murderer.*

Speaking of which: the title of *The Big Sleep* is realized in the last pages of the book. It's a slangy way of saying Death:

> What did it matter where you lay once you were dead? ...
> You were dead, you were sleeping the big sleep, you were not bothered by things like that....You just slept the big sleep, not caring about the nastiness of how you died or where you fell.

But the phrase "the big sleep" also suggests a sort of suspended animation, an un-wokeness, a perpetual bad-dream state, a walking nightmare from which all of us are trying to awaken.

How did Chandler put it? *Like a thought trying to form itself on the edge of consciousness.*

One day the thought will form. One day we will all of us wake up from the big sleep.

---

* Luigi Mangione

CHAPTER 12
INSIDE THE WHALE

AN ESSAY BY GEORGE ORWELL

January 5, 2025
Two weeks before inauguration

———

ONE OF THE wonderful virtues of owning books is that, as physical objects that adorn your shelves and not pixels on some flickering electronic device, they stand and wait, always at the ready, like spices in a rack, to be called upon. We never know when we may be inspired to pick one up, read through it, and extract from it the wisdom bound, literally *bound*, within its pages.

Thirty some-odd years ago, I bought a copy of *An Age Like This*, the first volume of George Orwell's collected essays, journalism, and letters, covering the period 1920-1940. Back in 1996 or so, I read the first few pages, got bored, and placed the book on my shelf, where it sat gathering dust until this week, when the great librarian of intuition pushed it into my lap.

Orwell's contemporary writings in the early days of the Second World War, irrelevant to me in my early twenties during the Clinton Administration, have, in the first few days of 2025, become exigent, urgent, vital. Here is one of the most prescient novelists of the twentieth century, an ardent anti-Fascist, revealing some of his thought processes in the years before writing *Nineteen Eighty-Four*, arguably the most important work of fiction of the last hundred years.

In 1940, Orwell published a long essay called "Inside the Whale," ostensibly an examination of the unexpected new direction English literature had taken while Hitler and Stalin were busy consolidating their power and, in so doing, imposing aesthetic restrictions on writers and artists. A lot of authors are discussed in the essay, but the main focus is *Tropic of Cancer*, the controversial novel by Henry Miller that was denounced as pornography when Obelisk Press published the first edition in 1934, and widely banned. (Want to read banned books? This is the book most banned! Not only that, but this is the book which illicit sale generated the ruling in *Grove Press v. Gerstein* that struck down book bans!) Indeed, Orwell's own copy of *Tropic of Cancer* was seized by British authorities in January 1940. As he writes to his friend and publisher Victor Gollancz, "two detectives suddenly arrived at my house with orders from the public prosecutor to seize all books which I had 'received through the post,'" adding, with no little irony, "The police were only carrying out orders and were very nice about it."

Curiously, I read *Tropic of Cancer* right around the time that I bought *An Age Like This*, oblivious to the fact that the latter contained an essay about the former. I quite liked it. Miller, it seemed to me, was living the sort of life the Beat writers, who I detest, aspired to live, claimed to live, but were not authentically living. (Like, for most of his life, Kerouac that big rebel *lived with his mom*.) Henry Miller was a literary party crasher. He was *metal*. I admired his ambition, his commitment to his art, his free spirit, his sense of adventure. (As far as adventure goes, I was, and am, a careful guy, more comfortable with the Kerouac living-with-mom attitude than Miller's devil-may-care drunken Parisian poverty.) I liked that he took himself and his work seriously. I liked that he demanded attention—but not in the plastic, surface way that, say, an Instagram influencer demands our attention.

This, the third paragraph of *Tropic of Cancer*, is a nice example of the "mad gaiety," as Anaïs Nin puts it in her foreword to the novel, of his proclamatory style:

> Boris has just given me a summary of his views. He is a weather prophet. The weather will continue bad, he says. There will be more calamities, more death, more despair. Not the slightest indication of a change anywhere. The cancer of time is eating us away. Our heroes have killed themselves, or are killing themselves. The hero, then, is not Time, but Timelessness. We must get in step, a lock step, toward the prison of death. There is no escape. The weather will not change.

I have tried a few times since to re-read *Tropic of Cancer*, but can't get past the first two chapters. It's too scattered, too haphazard, too precious, while at the same time being all about *him*. Nothing really *happens*, and a lot of his artistic pretensions are just that: pretentious. Although it teems with sexual vivacity—Henry Miller was a horny old goat—it is not particularly good pornography, or even good erotica. Miller is misogynistic, antisemitic, irresponsible, narcissistic, kind of an asshole, and a huge troll. One might even call him "Trumpy." But in 1934, his approach was revolutionary. Miller stampeded into the literary temple like an angry, profane bull and rammed his horns into the tables of the critics, overturning the apple cart of literature.

Orwell's sensibilities were hardly in "lock step," as it were, with those of his contemporaries; he was *sui generis*. Even so, he was not at all like Henry Miller. Eric Blair was a man plugged into the wider world: Burma, India, Catalonia, the seedier parts of Paris and London, and also Eton, where he was taught French by Aldous Huxley. (*Quel meilleur des mondes cela a dû être!*) Miller, by contrast, was a world unto himself, seemingly impervious to the global goings-on around him.

While reading *Tropic of Cancer*, Orwell is made acutely aware of this difference of approach. "Inside the Whale" is, basically, his attempt to reconcile his critical admiration for the novel—which is not, as he puts it, "a bit of naughty-naughty leftover from the 'twenties…but a very remarkable book"—and his personal disdain for the passive attitude of its author. He writes:

> When *Tropic of Cancer* was published the Italians were marching into Abyssinia and Hitler's concentration camps were already bulging. The intellectual foci of the world were Rome, Moscow and Berlin. It did not seem to be a moment at which a novel of outstanding value was likely to be written about American dead-beats cadging drunks in the Latin Quarter. Of course a novelist is not obliged to write directly about contemporary history, but a novelist who simply disregards the major public events of the moment is generally either a footler or a plain idiot.

A *footler* is one who *footles*: that is, a time-waster, a fritterer, a ditherer. Orwell recognizes that Miller is neither footler nor idiot, but struggles to comprehend his "mystical acceptance of the thing-as-it-is:"

> Only, what is he accepting? …[N]ot an epoch of expansion and liberty, but an epoch of fear, tyranny and regimentation. To say "I accept" in an age like our own is to say that you accept concentration camps, rubber truncheons, Hitler, Stalin, bombs, aeroplanes, tinned food, machine-guns, putsches, purges, slogans, Bedaux belts, gas-masks, submarines,

spies, *provocateurs*, press censorship, secret prisons, aspirins, Hollywood films and political murders. Not *only* those things, of course, but those things among others. And on the whole that is Henry Miller's attitude.

Orwell is not basing his opinion solely on the text of *Tropic of Cancer*. Eric Blair knew Henry Miller well enough to have dinner with him in Paris a few days before Christmas, 1936. He was on his way to Spain, where he planned to cover the civil war—the original anti-Fascist battle of the twentieth century:

> What most intrigued me about [Miller] was to find that he felt no interest in the Spanish war whatever. He merely told me in forcible terms that to go to Spain at that moment was the act of an idiot. He could understand anyone going there from purely selfish motives, out of curiosity, for instance, but to mix oneself up in such things *from a sense of obligation* was sheer stupidity. In any case my ideas about combating Fascism, defending democracy, etc etc were all boloney. Our civilisation was destined to be swept away and replaced by something so different that we should scarcely regard it as human—a prospect that did not bother him, he said. And some such outlook is implicit throughout his work. Everywhere there is the sense of the approaching cataclysm, and almost everywhere the implied belief that it doesn't matter.

This is, I think, a spot-on reading of *Tropic of Cancer*. Miller's original choice of title was *Crazy Cock*—yuck—but a better one might have been: *Atlas Shrugged at the Approaching Cataclysm*. The prevailing obscenity laws prevented Orwell from quoting from the book to show what he meant, but I don't have such prim limitations. Here is one such passage:

The world around me is dissolving, leaving here and there spots of time. The world is a cancer eating itself away...I am thinking that when the great silence descends upon all and everywhere music will at last triumph. When into the womb of time everything is again withdrawn chaos will be restored and chaos is the score upon which reality is written. You, Tania, are my chaos.

And this:

You are the sieve through which my anarchy strains, resolves itself into words. Behind the word is chaos. Each word a stripe, a bar, but there are not and never will be enough bars to make the mesh.

And finally, this bit of shiny happy fun:

For a hundred years or more the world, *our* world, has been dying. And not one man, in these last hundred years or so, has been crazy enough to put a bomb up the asshole of creation and set it off. The world is rotting away, dying piece meal. But it needs the *coup de grâce*, it needs to be blown to smithereens.

That last excerpt calls to mind another piece of writing, from half a century later:

It will be objected that the French and Russian Revolutions were failures. But most revolutions have two goals. One is to destroy an old form of society and the other is to set up the new form of society envisioned by the revolutionaries. The French and Russian revolutionaries failed (fortunately!) to create the new kind of society of which they dreamed, but they were quite successful in destroying the old society.

That's a passage from *Industrial Society and Its Future*, otherwise known as the Unabomber Manifesto—the seminal text of the neo-reactionary Dark Enlightenment.

———

A shorter word for "the implied belief that [the coming cataclysm] doesn't matter" is *nihilism*. Miller was damn sure familiar with the word and the philosophy. The term was first popularized by Ivan Turgenev in his 1862 novel *Fathers and Sons*; early in *Tropic of Cancer*, on page eleven in my copy, Miller extols "the perfection of Turgenev." Here is the (nihilistic) paragraph that follows:

> There is only one thing which interests me vitally now, and that is the recording of all that which is omitted in books. Nobody, so far as I can see, is making use of those elements in the air which give direction and motivation to our lives. Only the killers seem to be extracting from life some satisfactory measure of what they're putting into it. The age demands violence, but we are getting only abortive explosions. Revolutions are nipped in the bud, or else succeed too quickly. Passion is quickly exhausted. Men fall back on ideas, *comme d'habitude*. Nothing is proposed that can last more than twenty-four hours. We are living a million lives in the space of a generation.

That's rousing stuff, to be sure. But it is neither left nor right. It could be comfortably inserted into a Luigi Mangione manifesto or a pre-J6 speech by Alex Jones. There's no inherent political bent to nihilism.

All of this *après moi, le déluge* stuff is anathema to Orwell, who *does* believe in something (democratic, which is to say *real*, socialism; neither the Nazi nor Soviet variety). In

"Inside the Whale," he writes about the "debunking of western civilisation" that reached a fever pitch in the affluent twenties, with the result, by 1940, of a disillusioned generation hungry for purpose and meaning. "Patriotism, religion, the Empire, the family, the sanctity of marriage, the Old School Tie, birth, breeding, honour, discipline—anyone of ordinary education could turn the whole lot of them inside out in three minutes. But what do you achieve, after all, by getting rid of such primal things as patriotism and religion? You have not necessarily got rid of the need for *something to believe in*."

Yes! By George, exactly that!

If this nihilistic disillusionment was acutely felt in the thirties, before Google and social media, when the laughably benign *Tropic of Cancer* was considered so obscene as to be pornographic, what of now, when Western civilization is not so much debunked as drowning in content? We may believe in the same things Orwell believed in: democracy, anti-fascism, human rights, the rule of law. But at the moment, our politicians, our media figures, our celebrities, our plutocrats— our *leaders*; not all of them, of course, but far too many—seem unconcerned with any of this, seem blithely ignorant of the grim reality of our plight. We are believers abandoned by our gods.

What to do about that? Where to find our purpose and meaning? Or, rather, how to best *nurture*, best *harness*, and best *direct* our purpose and meaning, to achieve the desired result? A thousand violins playing at once demand a conductor!

This spiritual struggle is not peculiar to anti-fascists. Orwell notes that many writers of a hundred years ago took to Catholicism, seeking purpose and meaning in the oldest and most mystical Christian church. This is interesting when we consider that Catholicism is today popular among the aforementioned Dark Enlightenment set, and that a reactionary, Opus Dei-flavored strain of that religion commands much power in the halls of justice. (During the McCarthy hearings Jack Kerouac, one generation removed from Miller, got stoned and cheered for the bad guys; the King of the Beats was a staunch Catholic who painted a portrait of the Nazi-loving Pope Pius XII and hung it in his home.)

The two great midcentury novelists, one British one American, are responding to the same world problems, reacting to the same cultural and geopolitical stimuli, but in diametrically opposite ways—although Henry Miller is not, on the surface, much concerned about any of it. He loathes everything, not least the country of his birth, but he doesn't let it get to him. "America," he writes, in one of the more hyperbolic proclamations in *Tropic of Cancer*, "is the very incarnation of doom. She will drag the whole world down to the bottomless pit." Orwell's strong convictions Miller sees as—and because Orwell uses the word "idiot" twice in the essay, I'm guessing this is an exact quote—idiotic.

The feelings are perhaps not reciprocal. Orwell writes:

> At this date it hardly even needs a war to bring home to us the disintegration of our society and the increasing helplessness of all decent people. It is for this reason that I think that the passive, non-cooperative attitude implied in Henry Miller's work is justified. Whether or not it is an expression of what people *ought* to feel, it probably comes somewhere near to expressing what they *do* feel.

The disintegration of our society and the increasing helplessness of all decent people come part and parcel with the *establishment* of a *different* society (cut to the Unabomber, smiling) and the increasing *power-consolidation* of all the assholes (cut to Elon Musk, failing to smile like a normal human). Not nineteen eighty-four but twenty twenty-five. Is there not, among us decent people, a tropism toward passivity, if not obedience-in-advance, in these dark times? Is this

not how *we* feel, with the second Trump inauguration loom-
ing, just two weeks away? Don't we want to curl into the fetal
position and bury ourselves in blankets on the couch? Or is
that just me?

And so what if it is? Going numb is not the same as obey-
ing. Non-cooperation is not collaboration. Or, as the Gen X
filmmaker Richard Linklater put it back in the *Slacker* nineties,
"Withdrawal in disgust is not the same as apathy."

This inner conflict, I think, is what Orwell grapples with in
"Inside the Whale." He wants somehow to be active and
passive *at the same time*. Perhaps that ambiguity is what makes
conservatives and liberals both claim him as one of
their own?

————

The title of Orwell's long essay derives from a piece Henry
Miller wrote about the diaries of Anaïs Nin, in which he
compares his friend and lover to Jonah in the belly of the
whale, and goes on to suggest that, all things considered,
there are worse places to be. (Florida, maybe?)

"The whale's belly," Orwell explains, "is simply a womb
big enough for an adult." He continues:

> There you are, in the dark, cushioned space that exactly fits
> you, with yards of blubber between yourself and reality, able
> to keep up an attitude of the completest indifference, no
> matter *what* happens. A storm that would sink all the battle-
> ships in the world would hardly reach you as an echo. Even
> the whale's own movements would probably be impercep-
> tible to you….Short of being dead, it is the final, unsurpass-
> able stage of irresponsibility….

We detect a hint of wistfulness that almost approaches
envy when Orwell laments that, without a doubt, "Miller

himself is inside the whale." It's a see-through whale, to be sure, and it probably has a stripper pole running down from the blowhole, and certainly a full bar, but it's a big fishy safe space just the same. Orwell marvels at the fact that Miller "feels no impulse to alter or control the process that he is undergoing. He has performed the essential Jonah act of allowing himself to be swallowed, remaining passive, *accepting*."

Nice to stop swimming against the current and give in. But give in to what? Soviets and Nazis? Concentration camps? Great famines? And, further, what is the writer's duty at such a moment? Fascism is based on lies, after all, and fiction, while made-up, is based on truth. Is there—can there even *be*—a literature of totalitarianism? Orwell writes:

> Almost certainly we are moving into an age of totalitarian dictatorships….The literature of liberalism is coming to an end and the literature of totalitarianism has not yet appeared and is barely imaginable. As for the writer, he is sitting on a melting iceberg; he is merely an anachronism, a hangover from the bourgeois age, as surely doomed is the hippopotamus. Miller seems to be a man out of the common because he saw and proclaimed this fact a long while before most of his contemporaries….

And lo, smack dab on the first page of *Tropic of Cancer*, as if to end the suspense, Miller declares, "Everything that was literature has fallen from me. There are no more books to be written, thank God."

The beginning of *Tropic of Cancer* brings us to the end of "Inside the Whale"—the passage that has the most relevance to the here and now. We decent people are all, I think, struggling to come to terms with the impending Trump Redux. We've memorized our Timothy Snyder rules, we've leaned on each other more, we've deleted social media apps and canceled legacy media subscriptions and turned off the cable news shows. But ultimately we are trying to solve the same puzzle that, for a good long while, stumped George Fucking Orwell. In this passage, he has *synthesized* the two ideas: the *active* defense of freedom and the *passive* acceptance of tyranny. He's almost there:

> Progress and reaction have both turned out to be swindles. Seemingly there is nothing left but quietism—robbing reality of its terrors by simply submitting to it. Get inside the whale —or rather, admit that you are inside the whale (for you *are*, of course). Give yourself over to the world-process, stop fighting against it or pretending that you control it; simply accept it, endure it, record it. That seems to be the formula that any sensitive novelist is now likely to adopt. A novel on more positive, "constructive" lines, and not emotionally spurious, is at present very difficult to imagine.

Orwell finished "Inside the Whale" in 1940. By the time *Nineteen Eighty-Four* is published, nine years later, he's cracked the code. He's figured out how to be both active *and* passive in his fiction, and even, perhaps, glimpsed how literature can be both liberalistic and totalitarian. To understand this, we need only look at how he ends his last and greatest literary work:

> Two gin-scented tears trickled down the sides of his nose. But it was alright, everything was alright, the struggle was finished. He had won the victory over himself. He loved Big Brother.

That is Winston Smith—finally! after forty years of inner struggle!—allowing the great cetacean to swallow him up. He has gone the way of Henry Miller. At long last, he is inside the whale!

(It's hard to read the antepenultimate line and not think of Joe Biden, in his flaccid speech after the election, insisting that "we're going to be okay.")

Ah, but *Nineteen Eighty-Four* does not end with the story of Winston Smith. The last pages of the book are a curious appendix, "The Principles of Newspeak," which reads not unlike the other essays in *An Age Like This*. This is a faux scholarly text, an analysis of what the Party was trying to achieve with its modifications to the English language: "The purpose of Newspeak was not only to provide a medium of expression for the world-view and mental habits proper to the devotees of Ingsoc, but to make all other modes of thought impossible."

The firehose-of-shit, accuse-them-of-what-we-do strategy pioneered by Joseph Goebbels and employed by Steve Bannon, by Donald Trump, by Stephen Miller, by Speaker Mike Johnson, by Elon Musk, has, I think, the same aim. By appropriating the very words we need to articulate their crimes, the MAGA are trying to make it impossible for us to call them out. They have linguistically neutered our denunciations. They call Hillary Clinton a pedophile, which is a vile lie; but it has the affect of making the word *pedophile* meaningless, so when an actual pedophile comes along, and is almost invariably a MAGA Republican, the label has all the power of "I know you are but what am I." We can't call what Trump did with the Russians *collusion*, because he has blown that word apart. Any honest attempt to audit the election results will necessitate the use of terms like *rigging* and *cheating* and *stolen*, and the Trumpists have used them so much as to drain them of all literality. And, sadly, we have compared so many people to Hitler, and spoken so often of Nazis, that Trump's own, very real Hitlerian tendencies are largely ignored by the press, and real Nazis have come from Germany to kiss the ring at Mar-a-Lago with impunity.

The thing is, this doesn't work. The Bannon-Goebbels strategy is doomed to failure. Boris the *Tropic of Cancer* weather prophet is wrong; the weather does change. The path of the Seine is not, *pace* Miller, permanently fixed. That's Orwell's message in *Nineteen Eighty-Four*.

The existence of the appendix tells us that the totalitarian state described in the novel did not last. Ingsoc, or English Socialism, collapsed. Big Brother fell—and much sooner than anyone expected. Context clues in "The Principles of Newspeak" (the eleventh edition) suggest that it was released at least a decade after 1984, but before the first two decades of the twenty-first century, when the Newspeak translations of Dickens, Milton, and Shakespeare were slated to be completed—so around 1995, when the *Washington Post* published Ted Kaczynski's *Industrial Society and Its Future* and Richard Linklater was talking about withdrawal in disgust. That means the (fictitious) "Principles of Newspeak" came out about the same year that I bought (for real) my copy of *An Age Like This*.

Jonah may be trapped inside the whale, but he doesn't remain there. At the command of God, the big fish vomits him out. He then goes to Nineveh, and warns the citizens that the city is toast in forty days unless they clean up their act, which they do.

So: he is passive, as passive as can be, gathering his strength; and then he is active, as active as can be, using his strength; and this is how he saves the people who, as the Lord puts it, "cannot discern between their right hand and their left."

Peace is antithetical to war, slavery is not freedom, and there is no strength, none, in ignorance.

CHAPTER 13
THE LEFT HAND OF DARKNESS
A NOVEL BY URSULA K. LE GUIN

July 30, 2023
A year and a half before inauguration

———

I READ *Nineteen Eighty-four* in 1984. I was in sixth grade. It was the first "real" book I ever consumed. I was too young to grasp the nuances or understand the political allegories, but George Orwell's *magnum opus* left an indelible impression on me—not least because I shared a set of initials with Eric Blair's pseudonymous alter ego. For years after, I recalled characters, dialogue, and scenes of the book in great detail. I even wrote a song about it.

The mass market paperback copy that I read—bought at a book fair at Drew University—is now lost. It literally fell apart. I replaced it with a lovely deckle-edged paperback that Plume put out in 2003, for the centennial of Orwell's birth. Thomas Pynchon, the quirkily brilliant and reclusive novelist, contributed the foreword, which on its own is well worth the cover price.

"Prophecy and prediction are not quite the same,"

Pynchon wrote 20 years ago, "and it would ill serve writer and reader alike to confuse them in Orwell's case." He continues:

> There is a game critics like to play, worth maybe a minute and a half of diversion, in which one makes lists of what Orwell did and didn't "get right." Looking around us at the present moment, for example, we note the popularity of heli-copters as a resource of "law enforcement," familiar to us from countless televised "crime dramas," themselves forms of social control—and for that matter at the ubiquity of tele-vision itself. The two-way telescreen bears a close enough resemblance to flat plasma screens linked to "interactive" cable systems, circa 2003.

Twenty years later, of course, most Americans carry a miniature, portable two-way telescreen in their pocket, in those rare moments when the device is not in use. The *Gravi-ty's Rainbow* novelist goes on:

> News is whatever the government says it is, surveillance of ordinary citizens has entered the mainstream of police activ-ity, reasonable search and seizure is a joke. And so forth. "Wow, the Government has turned into Big Brother, *just like Orwell predicted!* Something, huh?" "Orwellian, dude."
>
> Well, yes and no. Specific predictions are only details, after all. What is perhaps more important, indeed necessary, to a working prophet, is to be able to see deeper than most of us into the human soul. Orwell in 1948 understood that despite the Axis defeat, the will to fascism had not gone away, that far from having seen its day it had perhaps not yet even come into its own—the corruption of the spirit, the irre-sistible human addiction to power, were already in place, all well-known aspects of the Third Reich and Stalin's USSR, even the British Labour party—like first drafts of a terrible

future. What could prevent the same thing from happening to Britain and the United States? Moral superiority? Good intentions? Clean living?

Something, huh? Wow, does that paragraph resonate a lot more now than it did when I first read it two decades ago. We might say that Pynchon in 2003 understood that despite the well-known warnings of Orwell (arguably the most famous fiction writer of the 20th century and inarguably a staunch Leftist who wrote that "[e]very line of serious work that I've written since 1936 has been written, directly or indirectly, against totalitarianism and for democratic socialism, as I know it"), fascism, like all ugly but pervasive trends from our halcyon days, was primed for a nostalgia-tinged comeback. Twenty years ago, he saw deeper than most of us into the human soul—although no one, not even the literary prophet who wrote *The Crying of Lot 49*, could have predicted the plump, orange, short-fingered, vulgar form through which the American strain of fascism would choose to express itself.

———

Written in 1968, published a year later, and set thousands of years in the future, *The Left Hand of Darkness* concerns a visit by one Genly Ai—who, despite having a name Elon Musk would give his child, is an Earth man—to the remote planet of Gethen. Ai is an ambassador of the Ekumen, the governing body of the known universe, and his task is to get the Gethenians to join the confederation. Within that framework, the story goes in unexpected places, eschewing the genre's then-prevailing—and male-author-dominated—narrative conventions. As Le Guin herself put it, "Its style is not the journalistic one that was then standard in science fiction, its structure is complex, it moves slowly, and even if everybody in it is called he, it is not about men. That's a big dose of 'hard lit,' heresy, and chutzpah, for a genre novel by a nobody in 1968."

The inhabitants of Gethen are human, but not the sort of human that Ai is familiar with. He is puzzled during the course of his stay by the sexual habits and the lack of gender distinctions. The Gethenians are ambisexual—what we might now call gender fluid. Le Guin used the "he" pronoun for all of the characters on this planet, but Gethen is a world of They/Them, a woke planet where Ron DeSantis's hateful politics goes to die. This, to me, is not prediction but prophesy, LeGuin the year before the Summer of Love feeling and extrapolating the collective human vibrations. The Gethenians have their problems too, all humans do, but they have the gender stuff figured out.

There's plenty of standard sci-fi content in the book. The ansible, for example, is what Le Guin calls the technological device through which interplanetary travel is possible. And like all great science fiction, *Left Hand* blends in elements of fantasy. In his original blurb, Frank Herbert extols the high quality of "the mythology, psychology [and] the entire creative surround."

Here is one short scene, late in the book, in which the narrator Ai and his fellow prisoners—one of whom has just died—are being transported across cold terrain:

Counting the corpse there were twenty-six of us, two thirteens. Gethenians often think in thirteens, twenty-sixes, fifty-twos, no doubt because of the 26-day lunar cycle that makes their unvarying month and approximates their sexual cycle. The corpse was shoved up tight against the steel doors that formed the rear wall of our box, where he would keep cold. The rest of us sat and lay and crouched, each in his own space, his territory, his Domain, until night; when the cold grew so extreme that little by little we drew together and merged into one entity occupying one space, warm in the middle, cold at the periphery.

There was kindness. I and certain others, an old man and one with a bad cough, were recognized as being least resistant to the cold, and each night we were at the center of the group, the entity of twenty-five, where it was warmest. We did not struggle for the warm place, we were simply in it each night. It is a terrible thing, this kindness that human beings do not lose. Terrible, because when we are finally naked in the dark and the cold, it is all we have. We who are so rich, so full of strength, we end up with that small change. We have nothing else to give.

The novel is full of hauntingly beautiful passages like this: wise, poetical, patient, tinged with melancholy.

Despite all the ample evidence to the contrary, I believe in the essential goodness of humanity. I believe in our collective intellect. I believe that when we work together, we can solve any problem. I believe in the triumph of the better angels of our nature. I believe that love will win the day. The name of my column is PREVAIL, not "See? I Told You We Are Doomed."

The simple, obvious truth is that you can't have light without darkness. *The Left Hand of Darkness* includes this short poem, in which the book's title is realized:*

Light is the left hand of darkness,
And darkness the right hand of light.
Two are one, life and death, lying
Together like lovers in kemmer,
Like hands joined together,
Like the end and the way.

---

* "Kemmer" is the means by which the creatures on her distant planet reproduce.

We will get through this. We always have. We survived 1860-65 and 1941-45 and four years of a mob money launderer in the White House; we'll survive this. We *shall* prevail. And we shall do so *together*.

CHAPTER 14

SEPTEMBER 1, 1939
A POEM BY W. H. AUDEN

January 26, 2025
One week after inauguration

———

HISTORY MOVES AT A GLACIAL PACE. In the eight or so centuries between the development of medieval feudalism and the French Revolution, the lives of most Europeans changed so slowly and incrementally as to be almost unnoticeable. The population was much smaller (as were the people physically) and spread out far more. "The world of 1789 was therefore, for most of its inhabitants, incalculably vast," writes the historian Eric Hobsbawm in *The Age of Revolution*. "Most of them, unless snatched away by some awful hazard, such as military recruitment, lived and died in the county, and often the parish, of their birth," and typically did not ever venture far beyond a day's journey of that place. "The rest of the globe was a matter of government agents and rumour." Those few newspapers that existed had laughably small circulations; even by the end of the Napoleonic Wars, most of the population could not read.

As a cyclist taking an arduous ride up a long mountain path every once in a while speeds downhill, so the velocity of history increases from time to time. But even then, change typically happens over a course of years if not decades. I speak of the Norman Conquest, the Crusades, the Black Death, the Hundred Years' War, the Age of Exploration, the colonization of the New World, the Thirty Years' War, and so on. Heretofore, the whole of the 21st century has had a similar vibe—of big, sweeping, world-altering global change, happening over the short course of a generation or two.

But sometimes, the god of history hurls a thunderbolt, and radical change happens instantaneously. One single twenty-four-hour interval indelibly marks the end of one era and the beginning of another. September 11, 2001 is one such example; when we say "9/11," everyone knows what we mean, and the day of the attacks represents a clearly delineated before-and-after: there is a *pre*-9/11 and a *post*-9/11. Another critical date, and one that will be much in the news two weeks from now, is November 22, 1963. And December 7, 1941, remains, as FDR memorably said, a "date that will live in infamy," all of the death and destruction that surprise attack portended expressed in a seemingly benign two-word shorthand: Pearl Harbor.

I'm sure I'm not the only American (or, indeed, the only citizen of the world) experiencing some creeping dread these last six days—as Trump Redux officially kicked off with a flurry of hateful, retrograde executive orders; corrupt, inept henchmen being confirmed by a docile, shit-eating Senate; and worrisome official appearances at "Pro-Life" events and disaster areas where POTUS threatened to withhold federal aid—that January 20, 2025 may wind up being another such flashpoint date. Not the insurrection, which after all was put down; not the 2024 election, which yet gave us two and a half more months to fight back (although our leaders chose instead to fold like a bad poker hand). The Second Inauguration is the Day of Reckoning.

The British poet W.H. Auden, who happened to be in New York when the Nazis rolled into Poland, saw September 1, 1939 as one of those world-changing dates. He banged out a Yeatsian poem about it, with the date as its title, and published it soon after. It is even more apt, alas, now. Swap "September" for "January" and revise the title, and what changes?

> I sit in one of the dives
> On Fifty-second Street
> Uncertain and afraid
> As the clever hopes expire
> Of a low dishonest decade:
> Waves of anger and fear
> Circulate over the bright
> And darkened lands of the earth,
> Obsessing our private lives;
> The unmentionable odour of death
> Offends the September night.

The "low dishonest decade" in this sense begins with the Rough Beast riding down his gilded escalator in 2015, foreshadowing our sad national descent into despotism. We would be hard-pressed to find two adjectives that more accurately describe our collective feelings now than *uncertain* and *afraid*. And yes, waves of anger and waves of fear, sometimes in tandem, are indeed obsessing our private lives.

> Accurate scholarship can
> Unearth the whole offence
> From Luther until now
> That has driven a culture mad,
> Find what occurred at Linz,

What huge imago made
A psychopathic god:
I and the public know
What all schoolchildren learn,
Those to whom evil is done
Do evil in return.

The culture driven mad that Auden cites is the German one, which came into its own in the early sixteenth century, when Martin Luther began the Protestant Reformation in the Saxon town of Wittenberg. Linz, in Austria—Österreich; literally the Eastern part of the German lands—is the hometown of Trump's hero, Adolf Hitler. An *imago* is a vision one sees of oneself (the word also refers to a giant, fully-formed insect—a clever double meaning). It doesn't take a genius, Auden is saying, to know that evil perpetuates itself.

Exiled Thucydides knew
All that a speech can say
About Democracy,
And what dictators do,
The elderly rubbish they talk
To an apathetic grave;
Analysed all in his book,
The enlightenment driven away,
The habit-forming pain,
Mismanagement and grief:
We must suffer them all again.

This stanza refers to *The History of the Peloponnesian War*, a contemporary account of the 27-year conflict between Athens and Sparta that began in 431 BCE, written by the Athenian general Thucydides. The "speech" is the funeral oration of Pericles, the great Athenian political leader, who addressed the crowd of mourners at the end of the first year of the war.

The address is considered a eulogy for Athens—which is to say, for democracy:

> Let me say that our system of government does not copy the institutions of our neighbors. It is more the case of our being a model to others than of our imitating anyone else. Our constitution is called a democracy because power is in the hands not of a minority but of the whole people. When it is a question of settling private disputes, everyone is equal before the law; when it is a question of putting one person before another in positions of public responsibility, what counts is not membership of a particular class, but the actual ability which the man possesses. No one, so long as he has it in him to be of service to the state, is kept in political obscurity because of poverty. And, just as our political life is free and open, so is our day-to-day life in our relations with each other. We do not get into a state with our next-door neighbor if he enjoys himself in his own way, nor do we give him the kind of black looks which, though they do no real harm, still do hurt people's feelings. We are free and tolerant in our private lives; but in public affairs we keep to the law. This is because it commands our deep respect.
>
> We give our obedience to those whom we put in positions of authority, and we obey the laws themselves, especially those which are for the protection of the oppressed, and those unwritten laws which it is an acknowledged shame to break.

Pericles extols the virtues of the men who built Athens:

> . . . what made [Athens] great was men with a spirit of adventure, men who knew their duty, men who were ashamed to fall below a certain standard. If they ever failed in an enterprise, they made up their minds that at any rate

the city should not find their courage lacking to her, and they gave to her the best contribution that they could.

Make Athens great again!

Joe Biden could go on stage tomorrow and give this next part of a funeral oration first delivered a millennium and a half ago word for word, and nothing would have to be amended (other than the fact that he would finally have to acknowledge that we are, in fact, at war):

> It is for you to try to be like them. Make up your minds that happiness depends on being free, and freedom depends on being courageous. Let there be no relaxation in fact of the perils of the war.

And for the Musks and Zucks and Bezoses of the world? Pericles hates their guts and (rightly) considers them pathetic, selfish cowards:

> The people who have most excuse for despising death are not the wretched and unfortunate, who have no hope of doing well for themselves, but those who run the risk of a complete reversal in their lives, and who would feel the difference most intensely if things went wrong for them.

But back to the poem. Auden tells us that the lessons Thucydides learned almost 25 centuries ago—in a great war between a democracy and a dictatorship—would have to be learned again, in real time, along with the attendant pain, grief, mismanagement, and banishment of enlightened thought.

Turning his attention to more prosaic matters, Auden surveys the dive bar, where he sees entertainment and drink papering over our collective terror:

Faces along the bar
Cling to their average day:
The lights must never go out,
The music must always play,
All the conventions conspire
To make this fort assume
The furniture of home;
Lest we should see where we are,
Lost in a haunted wood,
Children afraid of the night
Who have never been happy or good.

The bar is a fortress—a bulwark against the ineluctable encroachment of our unhappiness, our fear, and, deep down inside, in places we don't want to acknowledge, our innate capacity for evil.

This odd stanza suggests that people have different sides of themselves—night and day; dark and ethical—and walk about trapped in bubbles of their own, which cannot be penetrated:

From the conservative dark
Into the ethical life
The dense commuters come,
Repeating their morning vow;
"I will be true to the wife,
I'll concentrate more on my work,"
And helpless governors wake
To resume their compulsory game:
Who can release them now,
Who can reach the deaf,
Who can speak for the dumb?

And then comes the part that made the poem—and, indeed, Auden himself—famous:

All I have is a voice
To undo the folded lie,
The romantic lie in the brain
Of the sensual man-in-the-street
And the lie of Authority
Whose buildings grope the sky:
There is no such thing as the State
And no one exists alone;
Hunger allows no choice
To the citizen or the police;
We must love one another or die.

The last line is deceptively simple. *We must love one another or die* can be read many different ways: as a statement of objective fact, as an aspirational self-help-style aphorism, as a paradox, as a veiled threat, as a *fait accompli* that is destined to fail.

Then the final stanza, which calls to mind the "thousand points of light" referenced by George H.W. Bush in his own inaugural address:

Defenceless under the night
Our world in stupor lies;
Yet, dotted everywhere,
Ironic points of light
Flash out wherever the Just
Exchange their messages:
May I, composed like them
Of Eros and of dust,
Beleaguered by the same
Negation and despair,
Show an affirming flame.

The world remains in a stupor—now more than ever, perhaps. The Just—the "helpers" Fred Rogers talks about—

remain out there, operating in the gloaming, and always will. The light *will* pierce through the darkness. Our individual job, Auden suggests, is simply to keep the flame going.

———

Almost immediately after releasing the poem to the world, Auden came to regret it. He considered it "trash," and did not like its inclusion in anthologies. "September 1, 1939" was his "Piano Man," his "Crocodile Rock," his "American Pie." He was sick of it, embarrassed by it, incredulous that *that* poem, and that *one line specifically*, would be his lasting legacy—but it also made his literary reputation and underwrote his existence. Did he stop believing in it? Did he realize, too late, that in fact most of us *do* love each other but die regardless—or, conversely, that even those who hate meet their Maker (if not soon enough)? Did old age make him misanthropic, curmudgeonly, and bitter? There were verses he cut from the published version, in which he espoused faith in "educated man" to know better than to go to war. He quickly decided that that was bunk. What was it that disillusioned him? In the months that followed September 1939, Lord knows, there was no shortage of awful events to shatter one's belief in human decency.

Athens lost the Peloponnesian War. Sparta, with help from the Persians, won. Thus was democracy defeated by—uh-oh—an alliance of oligarchs and a hostile foreign power.

To ambitious and selfish men (it's mostly men), oligarchy has a certain appeal—in 431 BC and today. As Athenagoras puts it, in a speech recorded by Thucydides:

> It will be said, perhaps, that democracy is neither wise nor equitable, but that the holders of property are also the best fitted to rule. I say, on the contrary, first, that the word *demos*, or people, includes the whole state, oligarchy only a part;

next, that if the best guardians of property are the rich, and the best counsellors the wise, none can hear and decide so well as the many; and that all these talents, severally and collectively, have their just place in a democracy. But an oligarchy gives the many their share of the danger, and not content with the largest part takes and keeps the whole of the profit; and this is what the powerful and young among you aspire to, but in a great city cannot possibly obtain.

That is what today's American oligarchs want: all of the reward and none of the risk. Was January 20, 2025 the date when things shifted permanently in their favor—when the United States went from being Athens to being Sparta, when Elon Musk and Peter Thiel and the other goober overlords finally got the green light to take it all away from the rest of us? And why do so many Americans *still* walk around in a fog, oblivious to the swirl of change around them, ignorant of the ill intent of the oligarchs, in denial about the malefic character of our once and current President? Will anything— *can* anything—pierce the bubble? If plague couldn't, then *what*? And: once reanimated, will these Fox News zombies even be *capable* of admitting they'd been had?

For that, we look to a passage from a long poem by Auden, winner of the 1948 Pulitzer Prize for Poetry, which title is similar to the titles of Eric Hobsbawm's history books, and perfectly describes our current moment: *The Age of Anxiety*.

We would rather be ruined than changed
We would rather die in our dread
Than climb the cross of the moment
And let our illusions die.

CHAPTER 15

DOVER BEACH
A POEM BY MATTHEW ARNOLD

January 12, 2025
One week before inauguration

———

BORN ON CHRISTMAS EVE 1822, the son of a pious and prestigious headmaster, the poet and cultural critic Matthew Arnold is almost a caricature of the nineteenth century British intellectual, the stiff upper lip made flesh—brilliant, passionate, intense, patriotic, complicated, full of opinion, not unfunny but almost comically solemn, seemingly incapable of having fun, and tragically repressed. All of this is apparent by a short glance at his photo, which shows an avuncular but ugly man, with a broad forehead, large nose, crooked but kindly smile, oddly parted and pomaded coiffure, and facial hair that resembles neglected landscaping at the world's worst office park. He kind of looks like Shrek.

In his twenties, Arnold spent time on the Continent, where he waxed as libertine as Victorian mores and his own reserved nature would allow. He hung out with the novelist George Sand, whose work he much admired; followed the legendary actress Rachel Félix around Paris like an incel groupie, catching every one of her theatrical performances; and, in Switzerland, fell madly in love with a girl named Marguerite, whom he saw as the Beatrice to his Dante, and who, some scholars believe, was a figment of his wild imagination and did not really exist. When he came home from these travels, he got a job as an inspector of schools, got married (not, to his dismay, to Marguerite), settled down, had six children, and wrote about high-minded things until he died of a sudden heart attack at age 65. All of this informs his poetry, which teems with melancholy, loss, frustrated love, sentimentality, nostalgia, high-minded literary allusion, and a generally negative view of humanity. We can sum it up thus: "I was denied my Marguerite, therefore the world is unfair and heartless, there is no God, and I shall hurl myself into the abyss. Woe is me!"

Arnold was big on woe.

But for all of that, "Dover Beach," Arnold's best-known work, is deservedly on the short list of the most famous, and the finest, poems in the English language—not just of the nineteenth century, but ever. The poem has bored into me; there are certain phrasings he uses that pop into my head at random moments, as I'm puttering around the house, doing the dishes and whatnot. Even so, I am of two minds about what he's saying here, as I shall explain.

The poet begins, simply enough, by setting the scene. It is night, and he—and there's not much doubt that the narrator of the poem is Arnold himself—is by the sea, in a house at the beach by the White Cliffs of Dover. The tide is high, the reflection of the moon visible in the tranquil water. Across the Strait of Dover is Calais, in France; the night is clear enough that he can see lights gleaming in the distance twenty miles away:

The sea is calm tonight.
The tide is full, the moon lies fair

Upon the straits; on the French coast the light
Gleams and is gone; the cliffs of England stand,
Glimmering and vast, out in the tranquil bay.

Oh, and he is not alone in the room:

Come to the window, sweet is the night-air!

In real life, Arnold spent his honeymoon at Dover Beach. That was in 1851, the same year he wrote the poem (it wasn't published until 1867.) So there he is with his lady, beckoning her to look out the window and breathe in the sweet night air. Which you'd think would be, like, a romantic and happy moment—but no, it isn't, because Matthew Arnold is a Dour Mary:

Only, from the long line of spray
Where the sea meets the moon-blanched land,
Listen! you hear the grating roar
Of pebbles which the waves draw back, and fling,
At their return, up the high strand,
Begin, and cease, and then again begin,
With tremulous cadence slow, and bring
The eternal note of sadness in.

That last line comes out of nowhere, like a sudden tall wave knocking you backwards into the wet sand. That's one of the phrasings that pops into my head now and then, apropos of nothing: *the eternal note of sadness*. As soon as he gives it voice, we can almost hear it, a low rumble, like the down-bow of a cello ever-so-softly on the C2.

In his work, Arnold often uses the vastness of the ocean to symbolize loneliness and isolation. On the other side of the Strait of Dover, we may recall, is the forsaken love of his life, the   possibly   fictitious,   my-girlfriend-lives-in-Canada

Marguerite. Whatever initially triggers him, be it the sweet night air or the sound of the surf, our poet interprets what to most of us would be a lovely, intimate scene between two newlyweds as not just sadness, but sadness *that never ends*.

Chesterton wrote that, even in Victorian England, a time and place not much known for its levity, Arnold was "perhaps the most serious man alive." So we should not be surprised when, after totally ruining the nice moment with his companion at the beach house with his tedious brooding, he compounds the *faux pas* by bringing up Greek tragedy:

> Sophocles long ago
> Heard it on the Ægean, and it brought
> Into his mind the turbid ebb and flow
> Of human misery; we
> Find also in the sound a thought,
> Hearing it by this distant northern sea.

How many humans, I wonder, while walking on the beach, look out at the waves and immediately think of human misery? I'm not even sure Sophocles was that morbid—and that Hellenic wet blanket wrote a play about a ill-fated dude who killed a man that wound up being his father, married a woman that wound up being his mother, and was so upset when he found out that he gouged out his own eyeballs.

Next, we come to the stanza where Arnold catastrophizes his own depression. It's not just *him* who's on a downward spiral, you see. The *whole world* is going down the toilet, and it saps his faith in humanity:

> The Sea of Faith
> Was once, too, at the full, and round earth's shore
> Lay like the folds of a bright girdle furled.
> But now I only hear
> Its melancholy, long, withdrawing roar,

Retreating, to the breath
Of the night-wind, down the vast edges drear
And naked shingles of the world.

There's another line that sticks with me: *melancholy, long, withdrawing roar*. But the fourth stanza is the poetical money shot. This part is why "Dover Beach" is in all the anthologies:

Ah, love, let us be true
To one another! for the world, which seems
To lie before us like a land of dreams,
So various, so beautiful, so new,
Hath really neither joy, nor love, nor light,
Nor certitude, nor peace, nor help for pain;
And we are here as on a darkling plain
Swept with confused alarms of struggle and flight,
Where ignorant armies clash by night.

For a long time, I read the "let us be true" line as hopeful, where "true" means what it means when it modifies the word "love." But then I realized I was wrong. He means "true" as in "brutally honest." What Arnold's *really* saying is, "Look, babe, let's not bullshit each other." And then: "I know it seems lovely that we are here in this beach house on this moonlit night, listening to the sound of the ocean that's so relaxing, years from now Sharper Image will make it a standard setting on their noise machines. But I've taken the red pill, you see, and I know that's just an illusion. In reality, the world is a dark, cruel, awful place, and we are all *fucked*."

This insufferable Eeyore is so deathly serious, he can't even stop contemplating the sad decline of the world *while on his honeymoon*. This is depressing stuff, made more urgent when we remember that as he unleashes his litany of dread and despair, he is close enough to the White Cliffs of Dover to hurl himself off them.

"Dover Beach" is a young person's poem, filled with the same urgent desperation that animates Romeo and Juliet (the characters, not the play itself). Rejection, disappointment, bracing dose of hard reality: these are things that break one's spirit. How charming that in 1851, young men thus aggrieved were moved to write timeless poems about their woe, instead of subscribing to Joe Rogan's podcast, attacking women on social media, and becoming neo-Nazi meme-lords!

And, needless to say, those last eight lines are, alas, all too relevant to the current climate in the United States—a country Arnold much admired, incidentally. We may as well swap "America" for "this world" in the final stanza. Our second largest city and cultural capital is on fire, our media has will-fully rejected truth, our so-called leaders have capitulated one by one to the returning despot, and we await the coming of Trump Redux a week from tomorrow.

It's not just at night when the ignorant armies clash.

———

But what makes Arnold so fascinating is that he changes. He evolves. The lovelorn bard of gloom and doom switches from poetry to prose, and in so doing, finds his capacity to hope and rekindles his faith in humanity. He became a cultural critic—and not of the kind that our contemporary young American men so heartbroken might become. In a land of snobbery and class division, he was a staunch proponent of democracy, and he correctly saw that inequality—in terms of income, class, or sex—would be the undoing of Britain.

"What a strange religion, then," Arnold writes in an 1860 essay, "is our religion of inequality!" The rigidity of the British class structure he rightly sees as an obsolete artifact from a bygone age, and the root of all problems:

> [T]he great inequality of classes and property, which came to us from the Middle Age and which we maintain because we have the religion of inequality…has the natural and necessary effect, under present circumstances, of materialising our upper class, vulgarising our middle class, and brutalising our lower class. And this is to fail in civilisation.

In other words, the compulsion by the rich and powerful to maintain the ridiculous caste system engenders more greed and consumption by the aristocrats, a bourgeoisie growing coarser and cruder and nastier, and the poor bearing the brunt of the bloated plutocrat's avarice. As Arnold correctly notes, "the greater the inequality the more marked is its bad action upon the lower and middle classes." This is, of course, the kind of rigid class structure our current crop of artless American oligarchs, too many of whom came of age in the rigid and racist class structure of Apartheid South Africa, wants to bring back. Insofar as "Make America Great Again" means anything, that is what it means.

"The remedy," he makes plain, "is social equality."

Ever the aesthete, Arnold was also a staunch believer in culture. To him, culture was not just the hallmark of civilization; it was the *entire point* of civilization. Corroded culture he sees as a symptom of social inequality. The effete and "materialized" patrician class, he asserts, in that same essay, cannot "have any serious and fruitful sense for the power of beauty." The Victorian equivalents of the Trumps and the Zuckerbergs and the Musks "may imagine themselves to be in pursuit of beauty; but how often, alas, does the pursuit come to little more than dabbling a little in what they are pleased to call art, and making a great deal of what they are pleased to call love!"

Ouch!

Culture, Arnold believed, derives from "the love of perfection." Culture, he writes in *Culture and Anarchy*, with italics his, is *"a study of perfection,"* and all art is generated by the artist's "pursuit of perfection"—which is, when you get right down to it, "the pursuit of sweetness and light." He continues: "He who works for sweetness works in the end for light also; he who works for light works in the end for sweetness also. But he who works for sweetness and light united, works to make reason and the will of God prevail."

By contrast, Arnold argues—and he may as well be calling out Trump, Musk, and the artless MAGA by name—"he who works for machinery, he who works for hatred, works only for confusion. Culture looks beyond machinery, culture hates hatred; culture has one great passion, the passion for sweetness and light. It has one even yet greater!—the passion for making them"—that is, sweetness and light; that is, kindness and truth—*"prevail."*

———

While writing this piece, I realized that I had misremembered one of the last lines of "Dover Beach." I thought it was *And we are here alone on a darkling plain*, where "darkling" is a fancy way of saying "dark and growing darker." But it's actually *And we are here **as on** a darkling plain*. In Arnold's darkling view of the world, joy and love and light and certitude and peace and the relief of pain do not—like Marguerite, perhaps —exist. The one word he never uses, curiously, is *alone*. The plain may be darkening, the confusion sweeping, the clashing armies of ignorance and artlessness and stupidity and hatred causing the rest of us to struggle and flee. But it's *we* who are here on that plain. We, all of us good guys. We are *not* alone. And we will be true to one another.

And if we rewind the poem and read it again, keeping all this in mind, we understand that the sea remains calm and the night-air sweet. The eternal note of sadness we let in can also be let *out*. The tide that withdraws also returns, replenishing the Sea of Faith. And if we stay together, the ignorant armies will expend all their energy attacking one another, and the world really can and really will be new and beautiful and various, full of unironic sweetness and light: a land of dreams.

FURTHER READING

This book quotes work in the public domain as well as copyrighted materials that have been used under the fair use provisions of U.S. copyright law. Here is a list of cited works. I highly encourage the reader to seek out and read all of them.

————

- Abbott, Megan. "The Big Seep," *Slate*, 2018.
- Arnold, Matthew. "Dover Beach," 1867, and *Culture & Anarchy*, 1869.
- Auden, W.H. "September 1, 1939" (1941) and "The Age of Anxiety," 1947, Random House.
- Baum, L. Frank. *The Wonderful Wizard of Oz*, 1900.
- Chandler, Raymond. *The Big Sleep*, 1939, Knopf, and "The Simple Act of Murder," 1950, Houghton Mifflin Co.
- Dickens, Charles. *Bleak House*, 1852-3.
- Epstein, Julius J., Philip G. Epstein, Howard Koch. *Casablanca*, 1942.
- Flannagan, Roy, ed. *John Milton: Paradise Lost*, 1993, Macmillan Co.
- Herman, Benjamin. "The Debate That Won't Die," Radio Free Europe / Radio Liberty, January 11, 2012.
- Herbert, Zbigniew. "The Envoy of Mr. Cogito," 1993, Oxford University Press.
- Hobsbawm, Eric. *The Age of Revolution*, 1962, and *The Age of Capital*, 1975, Weidenfeld & Nicholson, Ltd.
- Kundera, Milan. *The Unbearable Lightness of Being*, 1984, Harper & Row.
- Lane, Anthony. "This is Not a Movie," the *New Yorker*, 2001.
- Larkin, Philip. "Aubade," 1977; "An Arundel Tomb," 1956; and "This Be the Verse," 1971.
- Littlefield, Henry. "The Wizard of Oz: Parable on Populism," the *American Quarterly*, 1964.
- Miller, Henry. *Tropic of Cancer*, 1934, Obelisk Press.
- Milton, John. *Paradise Lost*, 1667.
- Nabokov, Vladimir. *Lectures on Literature*, 1982, Mariner Books.

- Orwell, George. *Inside the Whale & Other Essays*, 1940, Gollancz, and *Nineteen Eighty-four*, 1949, Secker & Warburg.
- Pynchon, Thomas. "Foreword to *Nineteen Eighty-Four*," 2003, Plume.
- Thompson, Dorothy. *I Saw Hitler!*, 1936, and "Who Goes Nazi?" *Harpers Magazine*, 1941.
- Thucydides. *History of the Peloponnesian War*, ca. 410 BCE.
- Williams, William Carlos. "Asphodel, That Greeny Flower," *Journey to Love*, 1955, Random House.
- Zola, Émile. "J'Accuse…!" 1898, *L'Aurore*.

ALSO BY GREG OLEAR

FICTION

Empress: The Secret History of Anna K.

Fathermucker

Totally Killer

———

NONFICTION

Rough Beast

Success Stories of a Failure Analyst

Dirty Rubles